Changing Your Job

Godfrey Golzen & Philip Plumbley

Kogan Page

First published 1971 by
Kogan Page Limited
116a Pentonville Road
London N1 9JN

Second impression 1972
Third impression 1973
Second (revised) edition 1974

Printed in Great Britain by
Lowe and Brydone, Thetford and London

5BN 85038 360 9 (HB)
5BN 85038 470 2 (PB)

Contents

Preface to the second edition

1. **Facing up to change**   9

   When should you move?; The involuntary move;
   starting the search; Handling the transition period

2. **How to leave gracefully — and advantageously**   19

   Notice; Holidays; Redundancy; Scale of redundancy
   pay; Fixed contacts; Pension schemes; Ex gratia and
   severance payments; Tax position — redundancy pay
   and golden handshakes; Unemployment and earnings-
   related benefits; Supplementary allowance

3. **A personal stocktaking**   30

   What have you to offer?; Job satisfaction; Leisure;
   What are the limiting factors?; Identifying a course of
   action; A self-assessment test; What are you best
   equipped to do?

4. **Planning a job strategy**   53

   Job file; Surveying the market; Setting your objectives;
   An interview-getting strategy; A final word

5. **Making the most of your contacts**   69

   Business acquaintances; Top level contacts; Handling
   the meeting; References and recommendations

6. **Answering job advertisements effectively**   78

   The initial reply; Those forms

7. **Consultancies, agencies and others who can help you**   86

   Alphabetical list of consultancies and other
   organisations; Regional list of consultancies and other
   organisations

8. Résumés, application blanks and c.v.'s   124

    The telephone call; the c.v.; The résumé; The dossier;
    Application blanks

9. How to make an impact in the interview   138

    Planning the preliminaries; Making your entrance; You
    and the interview; The consultant's interview; Handling
    the interview; First impressions; The problem question;
    Will your face fit?; Negotiating the salary; The questions
    you should ask; Some basic interview etiquette; After
    the interview

10. Other methods you might encounter   155

    Psychological tests; Depth interviews; Group interviews
    or 'meet the board'; Behavioural exercises; Selection
    boards; Meet the wife

11. How to wait sensibly — and maybe profitably   164

    Put the word around; Advertise your availability; Use
    your overseas contacts; Check the agencies;
    Communicate your expertise; Keeping yourself
    up-to-date

12. New horizons   171

    Self employment; Franchising; Government; Lecturing
    and teaching; Opportunities in the Commonwealth;
    Opportunities in the E.E.C.

Appendix A: Writing 'on-spec' letters   185

Appendix B: Guidelines for preparing your c.v.   190

Appendix C: Specimen letter of application in reply to an
    advertised vacancy   191

Appendix D: Useful sources of information   194

Index of Advertisers   197

Preface to the Second Edition

This book is substantially an expansion of a work entitled *Changing Your Job after 35* which we wrote in 1971 and which rapidly established itself as the best-seller in its field. At that time the subject of executive redundancy was very much in the air and the book was produced in response to the fact that although there were numerous publications on job-finding strategies aimed at school and university leavers very little had been published on the rather different problems encountered by the man or woman who changes horses after some years in the saddle. It was also quite obvious from a number of TV programmes and newspaper features — as well as our own experience — that lack of an acquaintance with the techniques of assessing and marketing their own skills was causing difficulty to many otherwise perfectly competent executives on the move; accompanied in some cases, where redundancy had occurred, by the inability to adjust psychologically and even materially to being on the seller's end of the job market. The success of that earlier book, as well as comments made to us personally, indicate that the practical advice it set out to provide was both needed and useful; a point which is reinforced by the fact that it was the only "how to do it" book listed for further reading in the British Institute of Management's recent publication *Guidelines for Redundant Managers.*

Fortunately redundancy is now somewhat less of a problem — though it has by no means disappeared. But under the twin influence of economic policy on salary increases and the many new opportunities created by Britain's membership of the EEC there is now a great deal of voluntary job movement at all mid-career levels. In the light of this situation, the scope of the book has been considerably widened — there is, for instance, an entirely new section on self-assessment — substantial parts have been re-written and, of course, the information has been updated where necessary.

The authors would like to acknowledge the constructive comments, verbal and written, made by executives, consultants and professional institutes. Particular thanks are due to Mr. M.J. Hele, who has contributed a section on selection boards; to Mr. H. de Chassiron of Charles Martin Associates for his help on the original project; to Miss Nicola Kingston, formerly of the BIM, for supplying a number of factual items; to Mr. J.J.Q. Fox of Career Analysts for his advice on Chapter 3 *(A Personal Stocktaking);* to Mr. S. Morgan of the Franchise Advisory Centre, for his contribution on franchising; and to Mr. B. Eagles for his contribution on opportunities in the E.E.C.

Godfrey Golzen
Philip Plumbley

London, February 1974

Korn/Ferry Dickinson Limited

Executive Search Consultants

The long established firm of G K Dickinson Limited is now merged with Korn/Ferry International and offers British and Overseas Clients a truly international capability. Korn/Ferry International now have over 80 professional consultants engaged, full-time, in executive seach, based in 11 offices throughout the world.

Senior Appointments

Korn/Ferry Dickinson Limited specialises in recruiting well qualified men and women from a wide variety of disciplines for appointments carrying salaries in excess of £6,000 per annum. The Company is retained by a wide cross-section of leading British and International Companies and Organisations.

Method of Work

Each assignment involves a considerable amount of intensive library and field investigation. As background research material, extensive and up-to-date files on companies, industries and executives are maintained.

Changing Your Job

The services of the firm are retained by client companies only and the help it can offer to individuals is, of necessity, limited. The assistance however may be significant and senior executives who are thinking of changing their jobs may, if they wish, send us a copy of their Curriculum Vitae. This will be acknowledged and carefully compared with the requirements of current and future assignments, but will not normally lead to a meeting unless there is a close matching of experiences and qualifications.

Enquiries

To: Ronald B. Binks
      Managing Director
      Korn/Ferry Dickinson Limited
      20 Queen Street
      Mayfair
      London W1X 7PJ ENGLAND

      Tel: 01-629 7566

1   Facing up to change

Scarcely more than a generation ago people often made their career with only one employer. Today job mobility amongst executives is the rule rather than the exception. Indeed, in his book *The Age of Discontinuity* Peter Drucker envisages a time when, with the accelerating rate of technological and economic change, men may, at least once in their lifetime, change not just their jobs but their whole career.

That kind of drastic change of direction is still fairly rare, but most executives go through periods of restlessness after they have been in a job for a few years. Perhaps they feel that they are capable of doing more than they are being asked to deliver; perhaps the paths to promotion in their present set-up are slow or blocked; perhaps the money is not good enough; or perhaps they are simply bored with the prospect of doing more or less the same thing in more or less the same surroundings for the foreseeable future.

You have probably picked up this book because thoughts such as these have been running through your mind. But, as a man who is *choosing* to make a change, what has a book to offer you that is addressed equally to executives who have become or feel they might become the victims of change? Simply this. Whatever your circumstances, the principles of job-finding in mid-career are basically the same, and they are a great deal different and in some ways much more tricky than finding your earlier jobs ever was. At that time your salary would have been a great deal less than it is now, and your responsibilities in the company much less crucial. Now your commitments and expectations imply a position in which your salary is probably the least part of any loss your prospective employers might sustain if you 'don't work out'. At this point in your career, whatever your reasons for making a move, you have to prepare yourself much more intensively for the job-finding process than you did earlier on, because you are now trying to persuade some company or other to make an investment which in direct and indirect terms may run into hundreds of thousands of pounds.

When should you move?

Every step in this process involves preparation, analysis and evaluation and the executive planning a move of his own accord should begin by analysing the reasons why he wants to go. Apart from the fact that he should be clear in his own mind that this is not just a question of the grass looking greener on the other side of the fence, it is likely to be one of the first questions a prospective employer is likely to ask him. It would be difficult — even if it were desirable — to profile an ideal situation to move out of, but here are some questions you might ask yourself about your present situation.

1. Are your qualifications and experience being fully used where you are?
2. Is your expertise easily transferable or is it concerned with particular, specialised techniques that will narrow your area of choice?
3. If you have particular qualifications — e.g. a degree in languages — that you now want to apply, have you kept your hand in with your speciality or are you a bit rusty?
4. Are your salary and fringe benefits generally in line with jobs of similar seniority and responsibility that you see advertised?
5. Is promotion in your company to senior posts made mainly from within, or do they tend to look outside for fresh blood?
6. What job in your present company do you really want and is it likely that you would get it within an acceptable space of time?
7. Have you got everything out of your present job, or is there further useful experience you might still gain there?
8. When did you last change jobs? How many changes have you made in the last ten years? Progressive moves at three- or four-year intervals are a plus factor. But excessive restlessness or a long time spent in one job doing the same sort of thing will both need explaining

when it comes to the interview.

9. Would you really enjoy a change of surroundings and the challenge of doing something new? Without any other advantage or motive, money alone is a poor reason for moving, unless you are grossly underpaid (i.e. more than 15% out of line with similar jobs).

10. Would you be prepared to move to another geographical location? How would your family take it?

The last question is relevant not only to men who might have to move abroad — and this is likely to happen increasingly as trade with the E.E.C. develops — but to executives who are thinking of returning home after a spell overseas. There could be a lot of good reasons for such a move — personal and family ones, as well as the desire to get back to the hub of things in terms of of one's career — but after a long spell abroad broken by well-paid periods of tax-free leave at home there could be a tendency to lose sight of the realities of everyday living in the U.K. Salaries, for instance, are apt to be lower and taxation much higher than in many overseas posts; and those house prices you checked on your last trip home may have gone up considerably in the interval. Remember also that it is going to take time to find the right job unless you are exceptionally lucky and that in the meantime you are going to be living off capital. A careful assessment of such factors as these is essential, and they are dealt with more fully in chapter 4.

The involuntary move

Sometimes, of course, change may be wholly or partially involuntary. Employers, too, have to face the fact that a man who was right for the job when he was taken on a decade ago may not possess the range of skills and qualifications needed to meet a new situation. It can and does happen that changes in the market or in manufacturing will force a company to re-think the entire basis of their operation. A familiar example of this is the way a combination of factors — new methods of materials handling, the development of frozen foods, changes in eating habits as more people travel abroad, soaring labour costs and the popularity of supermarkets — produced a 'retail revolution' which called for a new breed of

11

managers in the field of food distribution.

Similar evolutionary changes are occurring all the time. Change is a costly business to keep up with and it also has the effect that big units tend to get even bigger. Thus small and even not-so-small concerns are squeezed by a trading and cost competition which forces them into mergers, into cutting back and rationalising staff, and even out of business altogether. Mergers in themselves often produce a situation where the new unit is forced to make a choice between two good men who have been doing the same sort of work.

All these factors are accentuated during periods of economic recession, which nowadays tend to hit managers and executives proportionately harder than any other group of workers. Government monetary policies force companies to cut back activities which do not produce an actual cash flow. Such activities are often marked by a high 'think' — and consequently executive — content: R and D, advertising, public relations and the pioneering of new products and markets.

Being out of a job is traditionally something that many executives have thought of as being somebody else's problem. Redundancy, or more brutally, the sack, rarely affected managers except the incompetent, the dishonest, or the desperately unlucky. That may have been the case up to ten years ago, but it is certainly no longer true now. A recent survey by the Institute of Personnel Management shows that only a small minority of jobless executives were dismissed for personal shortcomings. The rest are simply there because the climate for executives' careers has changed drastically since they embarked on them ten, fifteen or twenty years ago. The rewards are higher than ever. But the market for executive skills has become much more volatile and competitive. Companies, like private individuals, are more apt these days to chop and change and experiment with their personnel and this is a fact of life that one simply has to adjust to.

So if change is being, or looks like being, forced upon you, the first thing you must do is rid your mind of any outdated concepts you may have about being 'out of a job'. On the other hand this means dismissing any leanings you might have towards regarding redundancy, or the prospect of it, as something to be apologetic or defensive about or as a sign to the world at large that you have failed or been at fault. On the other hand, you should realise that whatever position you have held, whatever achievements you may have to your credit and however impressive the letters after your name, in today's circumstances employers are not going to be beating a path to your door. A concerted marketing effort on your part is essential to get your foot back on the ladder. This means that you will have to make a specific inventory of your skills, to analyse who needs them and to present them, in writing and in interviews, in such a way that an employer will be persuaded that even in a period of economic uncertainty you are going to be a worthwhile investment for him. This applies whether you have chosen change or whether change has picked you out. The principal aim of this book is to give you some guidelines, based on practical experience, on how to do these things effectively.

Starting the search

There are seldom any shortcuts through the long and wearisome process of filing applications and attending interviews; having made up your mind to move — whatever the reason — there is never a time when it is too soon to start your search. That an opportunity will fall into your lap is possible — you may be approached by a head-hunter — but the job you want rarely comes up when you want it. Many executives with a record of solid achievement behind them have received tentative approaches from other firms during their careers; the chief executive of a rival may have invited them out to lunch one day and said out of the blue, 'If you're ever thinking of moving, I hope you'll let us know'. That kind of contact will be useful to you, as we shall show later, but it does not usually mean there is a job being permanently held open for you at X's. Modern businessmen simply do not plan, or fail to plan, their manpower requirements in this way.

The man who thinks his job might be in danger is particularly apt to be a victim of his own illusions, and because he may only have a limited — even if a generous — amount of time in which to get resettled it is wise to be absolutely clear-minded about the realities of the situation. Sometimes such a man cannot bring himself to believe the facts, or if he does, he hopes they will go away. He has had ten or fifteen years' service with his company. He has a record of solid achievement in heading what he believes to be one of its important divisions. Surely they cannot afford to waste his talents? Surely, having given some of the best working years of his life to their service, they will look after him? It is not being cynical to say — don't bank on it. In such circumstances, you can reasonably hope for adequate compensation, but not that a post will be 'found' for you. Indeed, the more senior your position, the more difficult it is for the board to do this — quite apart from the fact that such jobs often disappear in the next stage of reorganisation.

Another common error is made by the man who sees trouble coming, who even maybe has taken to scanning the papers for jobs, but who feels there is no hurry. Every week there seems to be a lot of posts for which he is well qualified and which he would presumably stand a good chance of getting. So why rush out now? The situation may get better; he may even get an offer from somebody else if he drops a few hints around the place. Besides, he hasn't seen anything that's absolutely right for him yet. The fact is, though, that when he really starts trying he is likely to find things much tougher than he had imagined. It is reckoned by executive placement consultants that a man between 35 and 45 may take between four and nine months to find a new executive job at his level; and that the over 45s may have to spend as much as two years in their search, unless they are prepared to lower their sights quite appreciably. Even those firms that give what they consider to be ample warning to an executive who is to be made redundant seldom take full account of the time it takes nowadays for a senior man to relocate satisfactorily.

We are talking here, of course, of the executive who would prefer to stay where he is. Assuming you are in this position, at what stage should you make up your mind that the omens are definitely running against you to the point where you must start doing something about it? Once again, it would be difficult to profile a specific situation of this kind, since the

14

circumstances vary from case to case. There are, however, some situations that carry the seeds of a redundancy threat and among the commoner ones are the following:

1. It is generally reckoned that a man in a senior job in a company that is taken over is in an exposed position because the parent firm will sooner or later want its own protégés in policy-making areas. Executives who have been vocal in their opposition to a takeover are, of course, particularly vulnerable.

2. Mergers between two companies in the same field produce overlaps between services, such as sales forces, which are an obvious target for the rationalisation of personnel.

3. The closing down of a division, a part of an operation or an overseas office will affect not only the people who have been working in it directly but those who have been providing liaison and other central services.

4. A record of declining or marginal profitability in a company or division, particularly at a time of general economic pressure, may lead to closure or at least to a thinning-out of executive staff — even if they themselves are meeting the objectives they have been set within the general framework.

5. Close association with the policies of a direct superior who has been removed from office after a boardroom row often begins by making people concerned suspect to the new regime and ends by putting them in an untenable position.

These general signs will be accompanied, in the first instance, by a change of attitude towards the executive concerned by top management — or by his colleagues if he is on the board himself. Everyone is familiar with the horror stories of the men who come to take your carpet away, or of the executive who returns after the weekend to find that someone else has moved into his office. In real life, or at least in a civilised business climate, the signs are apt to be more subtle, if no less dangerous. The possibilities of signalling such situations are obviously legion but there are a number of familiar ploys.

1. Allocation to a special assignment or project which is

plainly removed from the real source of action.

2. Unexpected delays and barriers put in the way of obtaining sanction for necessary items of expenditure on staff and equipment.

3. The appointment of subordinates to your staff without proper consultation.

4. The appointment of an associate who, while nominally parallel to you, is in fact plainly enjoying a much fuller degree of management confidence than you are. This will manifest itself in such ways as his being called to attend policy-making meetings that you have attended regularly in the past.

Handling the transition period

Among the situations we have just described may be ones that you recognise as being your own. But if you are still working and have not been warned of redundancy one thing you must try to avoid absolutely is any sort of confrontation over the issues with which you are dissatisfied; because if there is no time at which it is too early to begin your job search, there is equally no point at which it is wise to endanger your present job until the moment when your next one is signed, sealed and settled. You may find your present circumstances humiliating and infuriating. Do not let this show in your attitude and do not complain about it to superiors, colleages or subordinates. Keep your problems to yourself (though you may find it a relief to blow off steam about them to an understanding wife or close friends) but in the office act as if everything was perfectly normal. Collect your salary and do your job as efficiently and whole-heartedly as you have always done. In the meantime look for a change with all the means at your disposal. As an executive you will not be accountable for every moment of your time, but when you have to go out for interviews make sure you more than make up for it by working evenings or weekends.

The fact that, for the moment, you are lying low does not make you a doormat. There will be a time to throw down the challenge about policy differences or a colleague with whom you disagree — when you have another job to go to if you lose the argument, not before.

On the other hand you may already have been looking for a job for weeks, even months. It would be insulting to offer you words of empty cheer in the face of the severe psychological (and often financial) pressures you are under-going, but it is worth asking yourself to what extent any of these problems arise because you have not yet fully accepted the realities of the situation. You have been aiming to get back at, or pretty close to, your previous salary and position. Is this, in the light of your age, qualifications, the state of the market, and the state of the economy, a totally realistic expectation? As a successful executive you have developed tastes and demands for yourself and your family that reflect your status and salary: a large house, a good car, holidays abroad, expensive clothes, regular entertainment, and so forth. Undeniably, it is extremely hard for a man to face up to the possibility that he may have to lower his sights to the extent of doing without some of these things; not only for material reasons, but out of pride and because, in an affluent society, we tend to see them as the outward symbols of one's place on the social ladder — and even, psychologically, as the marks of masculinity and success. But there comes a point when you should ask yourself whether you are attaching an importance to them that is not only born of assumptions that are in themselves open to question, but which stand in the way of your real need at this point — getting a job that will give you a position from which to fight back. Ability will out, and it is quality for which employers are always looking. With the maturity, judgement and all-round business know-how which you command you should feel optimistic about your chances of making your mark in any organisation you join, even if you come in at a level below what you have been used to.

Executives used to move only upwards or sideways — unless they stood still. The new factor is that you have to be prepared, on occasion, to move downwards as well; and that kind of manoeuvrability is difficult if you impose handicaps on yourself in the way of commitments you cannot bring yourself to give up even though they have no direct bearing on your actual career. This does not, of course, mean to

17

suggest that a former managing director should grab at the first clerical job that comes along. Not only should you beware of stepping down too far below your level but an interviewer might be suspicious of an applicant who was obviously doing so. But it does mean that you should be prepared to look at the possibility of a change in career — some suggestions for this are made in chapter 12 — at opportunities abroad and at jobs at a lower salary, often a notch down from what you had hoped.

Such a step, of course, involves you and your family. Indeed the whole matter of coping with redundancy is as much a family as an individual matter. Both from the point of your morale and theirs, the face you present in your own home is quite as important as that you present to the outside world. A general air of alarm and despondency helps nobody, and the best way both to get the family to understand what it is all about and to stop them getting needlessly frightened by what has happened is to look together at the family finances. Plan your budget in terms of a job search of at least six months and review it monthly. In this way they will see and understand the need for any material changes which you may have to make; and if you are seen to be keeping your head, they will certainly not lose theirs.

2 How to leave gracefully - and advantageously

There is a right and a wrong way of doing almost everything and leaving a job is no exception. Do so gracefully, because the very first step in your job hunt is to leave with the goodwill of your last firm.

If your search is beginning while you are still with them, it will help your morale and gain the respect of your associates if you carry on normally as far as possible — even when you are only working out a period of notice. Keep the hours you have always kept, and, if you are losing interest under the circumstances in which you find yourself, do not make this plain in your attitude to the job, your associates or the people working under you.

There will be occasions when you will want to attend interviews during office hours. When this is the case, notify anyone who may want to try and reach you while you are out. As an executive you will not have to account for your time; but, enjoying the status you do, it should be a matter of pride to make up in the office for any time you have spent in pursuing your own career. In certain cases, in fact, it may be an advantage to conduct your job search out of office hours. Formal interviews are conducted during the day, but if you are trying to arrange an informal meeting with a senior man who may have a job or a job lead for you, he is likely to have more time for you at the end of the day when the phone has stopped ringing. The fact that you are still choosing to devote all or most of your normal working hours to your present job may also be a fact that impresses him favourably. After all that is the kind of performance he will expect from you if you join his organisation or that of somebody to whom he might recommend you.

When the time finally does come for you to leave, circumstances have sometimes developed so that the temptation may be to go out in a cloud of steam, having told those of your superiors and colleagues responsible for your departure exactly what you think of them. However satisfying this prospect may appear, dismiss it firmly from your mind. For one thing your future employers will almost certainly check you out with your previous company before offering you a job. If you have left a bunch of angry men behind you, their recommendations are going to be less than enthusiastic. If, on the other hand, they see departing a confident, collected individual they will probably feel they made a mistake in letting you go. Ultimately this is far more satisfying to your ego than a slanging match, but what is more important is that the last impression they have of you (and that is the one they will convey to your next employer) is of a good man going.

To reinforce this point take some time during your last couple of days to drop in on all the senior executives of the company with whom you have had more than passing contact and say good-bye to them. Keep your comments cordial and positive, along the lines of the fact that you've enjoyed working with them and that you wish them success for the future (even though such statements may be slightly short of the truth!). Don't ask for recommendations or favours, and above all do not discuss the circumstances of your leaving. If you privately feel that there may have been faults on both sides, do not apologise for any mistakes you think you might have made. It is important that you yourself should recognise them, where this is the case, but keep such matters to yourself. What is past is past and should be referred to again only in helping you to build your future.

While your superiors and colleagues are important, do not forget those who have been working under you. Their loyalty deserves this token of your recognition, but, apart from that, the strong approval of a man's subordinates tends to register favourably with his superiors and equals. This does not mean that you should try and range your staff against the company or your successor — this will not do you any good and may do them a lot of harm; their liking and respect for you will be even greater if you do not involve them in your problems.

Leaving your job on good terms does not, of course, mean that you should leave without claiming all that you are entitled to by legislation and by any contract you might have with your company. Just as, in the course of your service, you will have attempted to gain the best possible terms for your firm, you should now make sure that you yourself get a fair deal from them.

In the first place your employer has a number of basic legal obligations towards you and you should begin by checking that he has fulfilled them.

Under the Contracts of Employment Act of 1963 the company should have given you written particulars of the terms of your engagement when you joined their service. The points in this statement that are of particular relevance to you now concern the minimum period of notice to which you are entitled, holidays, the provisions of the company pension scheme and any clauses that may set out compensation in case of severance.

Notice

In the vast majority of cases of executive redundancy, ample notice will be given, but it is worth pointing out that under the 1971 Industrial Relations Act any employee with 10-15 years' continuous service will be entitled to a minimum of six weeks' notice and that for more than 15 years' service this period should not be less than eight weeks.

You may be offered the alternative of either working out your notice or taking payment in lieu. The latter prospect is, on the face of things, tempting; firstly, you may consider that it will leave you absolutely free to look for another job, secondly, remaining with the company while under notice can be a somewhat humiliating and strained situation and, thirdly, because while you are working you are being taxed at your normal rate, whereas payments relating to loss of job (including ex gratia payments and redundancy payments) are tax free up to a total limit of £5,000. Against this you have to consider that it is generally thought to be easier for a man to find a new job while he is still employed and this was borne out in a recent Institute of Personnel Management survey. You also have to weigh up the tax advantages of taking payment in lieu against the fact that you will not be entitled to unemployment benefit until the period of notice which the payment covers has expired. In other words, if you are given four months' pay in lieu at the end of December you will not be able to start claiming unemployment benefits until the beginning of May.

Holidays

You should receive your salary for any holidays you have not yet been able to take, pro-rated on the proportion of the year you have worked up to the point you were given notice. You are not entitled to count as part of your year's work the period covered by notice. (See Tax position — redundancy pay and golden handshakes later in this chapter.)

Redundancy

In addition to holidays and proper notice, you may be entitled to redundancy pay — provided you have been continuously employed by your present employer for at least 104 weeks. The fact that you have been given payment in lieu of notice does not affect the entitlement. You should, however, bear in mind that you will only be eligible if you really have been declared redundant. The word is nowadays somewhat loosely used to cover the general state of being unemployed but in terms of the Redundancy Payments Acts of 1965 and 1969, such payment is only due if you lose your job 'through cessation or diminution of work of a particular kind in a particular place where he (i.e. the redundant employee) is employed.' You are not, therefore, entitled to redundancy pay if you are sacked or leave of your own accord. However, employers are encouraged to interpret redundancy as liberally as possible by virtue of the fact that the reason why the employer requires fewer employees does not affect the individual's right to be considered as redundant. This can be taken to mean that if you are running an operation that has to be closed down or curtailed because it is not producing results, your loss of office in such circumstances would count as redundancy, though of course whether it can be so described is at the discretion of your employer.

If, having been given notice, you leave before that notice expires you do not forfeit your right to redundancy payment provided you notify your employer in writing of your decision and that he does not object to your leaving.

Scale of redundancy pay
Compensation is calculated on the last week's basic pay, at an
upper limit of a rate of £40 p.w., multiplied by the number
of years of continuous employment with your current
employer up to a maximum of twenty years. There is also a
weighting according to age. The scale likely to appear to most
readers of this book is therefore as follows:
(a) For each year of employment between 22 and 40
     inclusive – one week's salary.
(b) For each year of employment between 41 and 64
     inclusive (59 for women) – one and a half week's pay.

Fixed contracts
Many senior executives have negotiated contracts with their
employers under which they receive benefits and terms of
employment running well beyond the statutory ones.
Inasmuch as these concern benefits in kind – use of a
company car, for instance – it is usually clear that these are
the property of the company, returnable once employment
ceases. A much trickier situation can arise over clauses
guaranteeing your employment at a certain salary over a
fixed number of years. In most cases such agreements will be
honoured, but if you are running into problems over this the
best step is consult your solicitor and show him the contract,
since legal documents are sometimes open to misinter-
pretation by the non-expert. What is clear however, is that
even if you are due to receive compensation under a fixed
term contract you are, in most circumstances, able to claim
redundancy payment as well. This will always be the case if
your contract was for a period of two years or less; providing,
of course, that you have been in continuous employment
with that company for at least 104 weeks. If it was for longer
than this, you will be eligible if the contract was entered into
after 6.12.65, and provided you did not agree in writing to
forego your right to redundancy pay.

Pension schemes
Unless specific arrangements are made in your contract for

the status of your pension in the event of your leaving the company's service, how generous or otherwise they choose to be is entirely at their discretion. All that can be said is that in the case of a contributory scheme, you may be entitled to receive your contribution back, either as a cash sum or as a paid-up policy; but in the former case, as you receive tax relief on your premiums, you will have to pay this tax back, though at a reduced rate.

Beyond this point practice varies widely, but most companies include nowadays, as part of the compensatory package to an employee who has been made redundant after a certain period of service (usually not less than five years), some form of pension provision. This may be a cash sum or a paid-up policy incorporating their contributions to the scheme to the time of severance. A paid-up policy will not be considered as a cash benefit for tax purposes, but an actual sum of money will be.

A paid-up policy continues to be valid, even if no further premiums are paid into it, but the benefits payable on the due date — either death or the time you would have retired had you stayed with your employers — only reflect the value of the premiums paid in up to the time contributions ceased.

If you wish to keep your policy going by continuing to pay premiums on your own account, you should discuss the situation with the insurers. But it should be pointed out that the financial burden is liable to be heavy while you are not earning (and therefore not benefiting from the tax relief which makes such policies attractive) and that it may be difficult to transfer a pension scheme from one company to the next unless the rules, levels and proportions of contribution of both schemes are similar.

Ex gratia and severance payments

Increasingly, companies are recognising the special problems of the executive made redundant in mid or late career by paying him a larger lump sum which will give him some capital to tide him over until he finds another job. This is based on such factors as age, seniority and length of service. It is not, of course, a statutory obligation to pay more than the amounts specified under the Redundancy Payments Act, so practice as to the sums involved and how they are based varies widely between individual cases and companies. It should be noted though, that if you are being offered more than the total you are due as payment in lieu, plus redundancy entitlement as laid down in the Act, you will not be able to claim under the Redundancy Payment Act as well.

Where a lump sum is offered to include payment in lieu you will have to watch that it does not prejudice your entitlement to receive unemployment benefit at the earliest possible date; because, as we have seen earlier, you are not, strictly speaking, eligible to claim such benefit until your period of notice has expired — even where, as is the case with most executives, it is longer than the minimum period laid down in the Act. Probably the best way of handling this is to agree with the employer that he should pay you the minimum notice as a separate arrangement while you are still with the company and that the ex gratia or severance payment should be a separate item payable after you have left their employ.

Tax position — redundancy pay and golden handshakes

See Income and Corporation Taxes Act 1970, sections 187 and 188.

Section 187 refers to payments on retirement or removal from office or employment. This section, in effect, states that you will still be taxed normally up to the last minute on such things as expenses, holiday pay, salary even if these are all given in one lump sum with a 'golden handshake'. It goes on to say, 'This section applies to any payment (not otherwise chargeable to tax) which is made, whether in pursuance of any legal obligation or not, either directly or indirectly in consideration of, or otherwise in connection with, the termination of the holding of the office or employment or any change in its functions or emoluments, including any payment in commutation of annual or periodical payments (whether chargeable to tax or not) which would otherwise have been made aforesaid.' This clause is equally applicable if such payment is made over to your wife.

Section 188 deals with exemptions and reliefs in respect of tax under Section 187. This is a long section and for our purposes two points are particularly relevant.

(a) Where payment is in respect of service overseas or the job requires the incumbent to be domiciled overseas and it amounts in effect to full time overseas employment (it excludes casual overseas employment of a short term nature only) it is exempt from U.K. tax.

(b) 'Tax shall not be charged by virtue of section 187 above in respect of a payment of an amount not exceeding £5,000 and in the case of a payment which exceeds that amount shall be charged only in respect of the excess.'

In other words this £5,000 is the total sum that is allowable. Even if split up into several payments over several tax years if it is 'in respect of the same office or employment, or in respect of different offices held under the same employer or under associated employers, this sub-section shall apply as if those payments were a single payment' and what is more the Inspector can choose which year to charge it under, which is unlikely to be to your advantage! So if you hold a number of directorships in a group of companies you cannot get away with £5,000 for each, even if it is given to you one year at a time. And if you are given the statutory redundancy payment in one cheque and a golden handshake in another it will still be treated as one sum. Or if you have your pension commuted (to give yourself some capital) this, too, will only be exempt from tax on the first £5,000 and lumped up together with any other ex gratia payment you may receive. Note, too, that if you are in a group you cannot avoid the £5,000 limit by being made redundant by each individual company in turn! So far as we can ascertain, the only way to get more than £5,000 tax free is to be made redundant by two quite unrelated employers within a tax year — in which case the Inspectorate may feel that you deserve it!

Unemployment and earnings-related benefits

You should be aware, for the purposes of the careful budgeting that will be necessary while you are out of work, of what you are entitled to claim in the way of benefits.

There is a feeling among some executives that it is

demeaning to accept aid from the state, and certainly the conditions in which this is usually administered and the whole circumstance of rubbing shoulders with fellow-claimants who are often, to say the least, a pretty mixed lot, can be a blow to one's pride. On the other hand there is really no rational basis for such an attitude. No one feels embarassed about accepting the benefits of the National Health Service (often under similar circumstances!) One pays national insurance, as one pays health insurance, for precisely the same reason that one may one day find oneself in the position of having to claim benefit from it. It is no more rational not to collect it than it would be to fail to claim from an insurance company after a motor car accident.

There is also another factor to bear in mind. If you are unemployed, but do not register as such, you will have to pay the Class 3 National Insurance Stamp for non-employed persons — £1.56 a week from January 1974. Of course, you will have to pay the stamp until you actually become eligible for unemployment benefit.

The amounts you are entitled to are not large, but they are useful; and if, having left it, you decide you need the money after all, it will be almost impossible to make a retroactive claim. Therefore you would be well advised to go to an employment exchange as soon as you become unemployed, bringing your national insurance card and your last Certificate of Pay and Tax Deducted (Form P60). You will then be informed of when you are able to claim payment and how much you are entitled to. The date when payment commences will not be affected by redundancy pay, but it will be affected by any payment you have received in lieu of notice or in compensation for cancellation of a fixed term contract.

The terms, conditions and amounts of benefit are spelled out in detail in leaflets NI 12 and NI 155A issued by the Department of Health and Social Security. But in essence, the weekly rates of benefit there set out are as follows (valid from December 1973 onwards):

Flat Rate	£7.35
Dependants — for one dependant adult	£4.55

Dependants — for the first dependant child   £2.30
            for the second dependant child   £1.40
            for each other dependant child   £1.30

In the case of an unmarried man an adult dependant may be a close dependant relative other than his wife. Children, in order to qualify as dependants, have to be either

(a) Under the minimum school-leaving age, or
(b) Receiving full-time education at school, college or university and under the age of 19, or
(c) Over the age of 16 but unable to work owing to disability or a prolonged period of illness.

If your wife is working you will not be entitled to claim for her as a dependant adult. But her salary does not prejudice any claim for yourself and your children, even if it is actually greater than the amount of benefit to which you are entitled.

In addition to unemployment benefit you are entitled to collect earnings-related benefit. This is scaled according to average weekly earnings in the £10-£42 range (the latter figure being the maximum level to which the benefit is related); and in support of your claim you will need to produce your last Certificate of Pay and Tax Deducted. The scale of amounts paid is roughly one-third of the amount by which average earnings exceed £10, up to a limit of £30, and 15% of earnings between £30 and £42. For an executive, who can be reckoned to have been earning well over this, the benefit would, therefore, not exceed £8.47. The supplement begins to be paid on the 13th day of unemployment and continues for up to 156 days, not counting Sundays.

It is easy to see from these figures that an unemployed executive with two children is eligible to collect a weekly benefit of £24.07, not a lot of money, but a very helpful subsidy towards the household expenses. Nor need you feel that as a condition of receiving unemployment benefit you will be obliged to take any job the labour exchange offers you. It is specifically stated by the D.H.S.S. that an offer of employment regarded by them as 'suitable' is 'employment in your usual occupation.'

Supplementary allowance

Neither unemployment benefit, nor earnings-related benefit runs indefinitely. In fact payment expires after 312 and 156 days respectively (excluding Sundays) and you cannot reactivate your eligibility until you have worked for a period of 13 continuous weeks. While it is hoped that most readers do secure employment within the prescribed period, there is a further source of financial aid to which you can turn — the so-called Supplementary Allowance. The circumstances under which it may be paid are set out in *The Supplementary Benefits Handbook* (H.M.S.O. 32½p).

The D.H.S.S. which is responsible for administering supplementary benefits, lays down that these are to be paid to persons whose resources have fallen below their requirements. A figure has been set on some of the latter. Thus, a man and wife are reckoned to need £11.65 a week for subsistence, with an additional sum for each child, ranging from £5.70 for the older ones to £2.05 for the younger. Allowances are also made to cover essential outgoings such as rent, mortgage, heating, light etc. No fixed sum has been set for these — the merits of each individual case is decided on the basis of an interview at the local social security office, in which such things as the possession of realisable capital are taken into account. This is assumed to produce a notional income, though the possession of an owner-occupied house is not counted as capital. An award is then made to bring the applicant's resources — in practice his weekly income — up to his requirements.

In some cases, it is likely that a former executive's claim for supplementary benefits would come under close scrutiny — particularly as he may be living in a better house than the official investigating his claim. The status, or former status, of an applicant is, however, quite beside the point, and if he qualifies for supplementary benefit he should press his claim — if necessary by means of an appeal to 'The Clerk, Supplementary Benefits Appeal Tribunal' at the local D.H.S.S. office within 21 days of refusal or an unsatisfactory award having been made.

3   A personal stocktaking

Looking for a job is essentially a marketing operation. As such, it begins by making an assessment of the product: what it can and cannot do, to whom it appeals, what features should be emphasised to potential buyers, where the best outlets for it are, how much the customer is willing to pay for it and what price the producer must charge in order to keep going. Perhaps you have never thought of yourself in this light, but as an executive you do, after all, represent an investment for the company that is going to employ you — a sizeable investment that can be very profitable if it works and disastrously expensive if it does not. To put the situation in its crudest terms, what it involves is being able to sell yourself; and any salesman will tell you that the man who can walk into a client's office with a thorough knowledge of his product and a clear idea how it is going to benefit the buyer stands a far better chance of success than the man who has not taken the trouble to equip himself with this knowledge.

Of course, an executive is not some inanimate product and there is, too, another factor in this process of self-assessment that you now have to undertake. Once people have settled down in a career, around the age of 35, they tend to rub along without thinking too closely about whether or not they are making the best use of their abilities in the job they have chosen. It may be that somewhere along the line you took, or drifted into the wrong decision.

This is a unique opportunity to take stock of your qualifications, talents and personal attributes and to see whether you have been applying them in the area that is right for you — or whether the fact that you have not been doing this is in itself a contributory cause of your redundancy. In other words, you have to challenge every premise on which your career thinking has been based, and start from there.

This involves sizing up your strengths and weaknesses, your physical and psychological needs, to what extent your personal circumstances dictate or suggest the kind of job you should go for, where you want to live and where you could bear to live, if necessary. It involves a survey of your experience and qualifications and a clear-sighted — even ruthless — assessment of yourself as a person. All this is a necessary preliminary in deciding what sort of job you should go for.

What is the best way to do this? We suggest you look at yourself dispassionately and analytically by asking yourself the following questions

(a) What have I to offer? Look at your qualifications, the course of your working life, your personal characteristics and how you interact with others.

(b) What sort of things do I actually enjoy doing — and how important to me is my leisure?

(c) What are my commitments in terms of finance and location?

Then, on the basis of these factors, identify a course of action.

What have you to offer?

To make an honest assessment of yourself is notoriously difficult. The best way is to come up with something that is meaningful and constructive — as opposed to the haphazard collection of illusions, and maybe self-accusations that are probably in your mind at this moment. Start with the facts. Take a sheet of paper and write down your answers to the following.

Qualifications and training

How well have you done at school, at university, or at other courses? Is your ability broad, or confined to one area? Are you essentially an arts man or a scientist or applied technologist? Even if after you left school you were brought up in what some people call 'the university of life' you should have some pointers about the kind of things you tended to be good at — like a gift for maths. If you are a graduate you will know what class of degree you were awarded. The fact that you received a 2.2 Honours does not necessarily mean that all your work was at that level. In some subjects you might have been good enough to earn a first, had you specialised in that area; in others you might only have earned a third.

From these facts you are going to be able to draw certain conclusions that have a bearing on your job search. It is obviously unlikely that you are going to want to branch out in a completely new direction, but now is your chance to make what astronauts call a 'corrective burn' to put yourself back on course. For instance, if you have a qualification in languages that you have never had a chance to use, a job which involves travelling abroad in a field of business in which you already have some experience may make you exactly the man a lot of employers are looking for. Equally, if your previous job involved accounting, quantifying or, on the other hand, communicating skills which you found it difficult to cope with, you should now be thinking about a post which is better suited to the natural leanings and abilities which your educational qualifications suggest. If you are thinking about a complete switch which involves taking time out to attend courses for re-training, consider how much receptivity you display towards learning something new. A clue to this will be found in your performance on courses you have attended recently and how successfully you tackle new and unfamiliar types of work.

The subject of 'courses' takes one into a field that is increasingly important for the training of the executive of today. How up-to-date are you, you should ask yourself, with your profession or managerial skill? The hard fact is that a lot of men, once they think they have established themselves, cease to bother to learn — or maybe they simply do not have the time. If you fall into this category, you should note the fact as a deficiency and look at possibilities to put it right. If you have been keeping yourself up-to-date, jot down the areas in which your special knowledge lies.

Service record
If you are over 35 you will probably have spent some time in the services. A good service record is an asset and contacts you

have made during the time can be useful, since the circumstances of service life form a tie that can be stronger than many others. But its importance should not be overplayed. Commissions were not that hard to come by, either during the war or in the years of national service and they are not in themselves a sign of leadership or any particular quality. On the other hand, your service life is certainly a part of the whole picture you are building of your abilities, and may have tested, for the first time in your life, such important matters as the ability to lead men and to get on with people from a wide variety of different backgrounds. It goes without saying, of course, that the importance of your service life is on quite a different scale if you spent a significant part of it as a regular officer, in which case such matters as the appointments and rank you held, and whether or not you went through Staff College, are all very much to the point.

Your working life
Now we come to the heart of the exercise – your adult working life. Make a list of the jobs you have held. How long were you in each one? What was your starting and finishing salary? Why did you move? When you were promoted, did promotion come more rapidly in some kinds of positions than others? Did you ever move sideways to gain more experience, or even leave a well-paid job with limited prospects for one that was less well-paid but seemed to offer a greater challenge?

What is the range and depth of your practical work experience and how transferable is it? Are there any major gaps? (It is easy to fall into one of two extremes here: either to think you are expert in everything because you have a smattering of most aspects of your function or to undervalue your experience as common sense.)

Be specific about what your various jobs and positions entailed. Apart from focusing your mind on the sort of things for which you have an aptitude, it will also help you to answer questions from potential employers in later stages of the job search. Don't simply write down that you were in charge of a department of fifty people, but describe the exact nature of your of your responsibilities, who you reported to, how the success of the job was measured and what your achievements were during the time you filled it. Did you, for instance, increase turnover while keeping overheads down? Did you introduce new systems of financial control or streamline and simplify an existing system? Did you carry significant responsibilities in helping to implement your company's changes of policy or procedure — putting through a new wage payment system, or helping to supervise a changeover from manual to computerised methods? Did you gain experience of specific new products and processes? Did you represent your company in any significant negotiations with outside bodies? Did you speak publicly on their behalf?

In his book *The Effective Executive* Peter Drucker says in consultancy assignments he tends to evaluate the quality of a firm's executives by their ability to answer such questions as these. They differentiate the man who knows and thinks about what he is doing from the one who is only going through the motions. It is a fair bet that your future interviewer will be making the same kind of judgement when he questions you about your previous record and that he will be impressed if you can give him precise, well thought-out answers.

But of course at this stage you are not yet aiming at a specific job, but rather building up a profile of the kind of job you would be likely to do well. An essential part of this process is to look at weaknesses as well as strengths. There is no need to be ashamed of admitting the former to yourself. We all have them, but the important thing is to find a job that will give the maximum opportunity to one's strong suits and make as little call as possible on weaker areas.

Here again your performance in various kinds of jobs will provide most of the clues, and you should do some hard thinking about the reasons for your successes and failures. Did you, for instance, do a superb job selling your company's products and services but perform rather less well when you were promoted to a managerial function? If this was so, it might indicate that administrative staff work is not really your line, or maybe that you are essentially a 'lone wolf' operator who finds it irksome to be organising other people.

On the other hand, you may have made an unsuccessful move from an office job to sales and have found that the give-and-take of direct contact with customers and clients does not come so easily to you; or your last job may have meant involvement with a kind of product with which you were not at ease. Although all kinds of business activity are more or less the same in their basic principles, in some areas, such as sales, a man who spent half his working life in consumer goods is liable to find the switch to, say, capital equipment quite bewildering. So what you should try and do is to use the wisdom of hindsight to identify the kind of job at which you were successful and happy.

What sort of person are you?

How well you performed as an executive and in what capacity you are most effective is not related only to your intellectual grasp or the depth of your qualifications. It is also a matter of what sort of person you are, as this is an important aspect of the process of self-assessment. It is also a tricky one in which you can easily end up with a useless list of highly subjective evaluations. The best way to approach it is to consider yourself in action. What types and levels of people can you mix with freely, intimately or occasionally? Visualise yourself in a typical business/management/board meeting; dealing with customers, staff or workpeople; at home, at the club. Try to distinguish the type of role you tend to take or to gravitate to and the attributes other people ascribe to you. For example, in formal situations such as at work you may be valued mostly for your technical expertise; but this may be because you have never had the opportunity yet to show that you have the requisite skills for general management; on the other hand you may be a very successful chairman of the parish council in your home village and people look to you for the lead in informal situations. What is your own style of management? Are you people or production oriented? Do you lead, drive or arbitrate? Who decides? Try to recall what other people have said or written about your dealings with staff. Can you influence your fellow directors; if so in what type of situation or issue? Can you influence other line managers over whom you have no

35

authority? How are you regarded in the Boardroom; as a technical expert? Or as a man with a good analytic brain? Or as a shrewd negotiator in face-to-face situations? Or as the chap the unions will listen to? As a maverick?

In the social or sports club do you tend to be secretary, chairman, treasurer or member? Even your family life has some bearing on the question. Are you authoritarian, or tolerant and easy-going? Psychologists view people in behavioural terms — the way in which an individual tends to behave in certain types of situations can be predicted from his behaviour in another set of analogous circumstances. That should be the aim of this stage of your self-assessment. Thus if you are basically a shy, sensitive person — no matter how well you have learned to compensate for it — avoid sales; you are unlikely to succeed there. If you can't take tough decisions about people without lying awake at night you should think twice about going into a job which involves a strong element of hiring and firing. If you work best at a job which involves a lot of variety, you will not be happy doing something which means intense concentration on one task over a long period. Are you, in general terms, intellectual, practical, physically active, decisive or cautious? Are you outgoing, or a bit of a loner? Are you creative or analytical? All these attributes (and you will be able to think of many others in connection with yourself) can be an asset; they can also be a disadvantage. It is up to you to identify the situation in which the former will hold true.

Interaction with other people
The question of relationships with colleagues is one you should look at carefully. Every worthwhile business organisation is ultimately dedicated to making a profit but most of them have their own style in the way they set about it and attract people who fit that style. Some, for instance, pride themselves on their informality, so that a person with a somewhat conventional outlook on things may come to feel out of place. The reverse is also true. A man who regards the niceties of dress and conventional behaviour as being of secondary importance to doing a good job is unlikely to be taken on by an organisation which favours white shirts and

hair short back and sides. So you should now consider your appearance, speech and manner. Show as 'strengths' the types and levels of people to whom you are readily acceptable; as 'limitations' those who, from experience tend to reject you; you should also note any factors relevant in social situations such as a stammer or a rough accent. The fact that some attribute or other makes it unlikely that you will get on well with certain individuals or groups of people is not necessarily a disadvantage, but to a potential employer or interviewer it will be important, one way or the other. Your accent, for instance, would not matter in the slightest if you were applying for a job as a works manager, but it might affect your eligibility for a post involving high-level negotiations.

But while, in the much freer society we nowadays live in, externals are, on the whole less important than they used to be, the basic currency of human relationships remains the same. In other words, there are still fools who occasionally have to be borne gladly, touchy superiors (not to mention superiors' wives) to be humoured and a lot of individual foibles to be handled with tact. Failure to cope with this sort of thing is often the underlying cause of an executive's wanting or being asked to move on, and while one's natural reaction in such a situation is to blame the unreasonableness of others there are usually lessons to be learned for oneself.

Job satisfaction

If you're not in it for the fun, what the hell are you doing here anyway? So asks the author of that engagingly outrageous book *Up the Organisation,* by way of saying that job satisfaction is a vital factor in doing anything well and successfully. So look back over the jobs you have done and decide which activities have given you the most satisfaction and which the least. It need not have been the total job you found interesting; it may have been one assignment, such as planning a new system of distribution, writing a set of sales brochures, or determining the lay-out of a production process. Now that you have got several years of experience of work it is relatively easy to discern a pattern and to work out its implications for your full-time occupation. This is impossible for the 21-year old to do – which is why so many go off course in their early days in business.

Your leisure activities will also give you valuable clues to the source of job satisfaction. The reason why any vocational guidance test battery will include an interest questionnaire is because, where it is possible to combine a deep interest with a job activity, the performance of the individual concerned will invariably be high.

Leisure

It is, of course, only the fortunate minority who can combine their job with an abiding private interest. For many indeed, pursuits such as sport, music, drama, painting or simply pottering about with the family are a necessary relief from their working life. On the other hand, there is the phenomenon that although the broad mass of the working population are enjoying more leisure than ever before, executives are actually having to work harder and under greater pressure. Whether it is a healthy thing or not, either from the individual's point of view or from that of his firm, the tendency is for senior, highly-paid jobs to involve long hours and often work over weekends. Are you prepared to make this sacrifice? Are your wife and family? Leisure and time spent with your family will have a certain value to you; and if you don't budget for it, you may overlook a vital physical and psychological need.

What are the limiting factors?

At this stage it is easy to get carried away by what you could do — in theory. But by the time most people have passed their mid-thirties they will have acquired commitments that are bound to limit their freedom of action. First of all, the question of salary. This is discussed in more detail in the next chapter but at this stage you should decide what your essential financial obligations are. There is a kind of Parkinson's law by which expenditure rises to meet income, so that a man earning, say, £7,000 a year, generally feels no better off than when he was earning half that amount because he acquires new tastes and thinks of new ways of spending money. What you have to decide now is which items of expenditure you are unwilling to give up except as a last resort, which you would be willing to contemplate abandoning and which are really quite incidental to your well-being. Everyone has his own scale of priorities — one man might think of taking his children away from a fee-paying school, whereas another would rather do without a family holiday — but the essential thing is to be aware of where expenditure could be reduced if necessary.

The other main constraint concerns location. The decision to uproot oneself and one's family is always a very difficult one, but you may well be faced with making a decision about which it is you want most — to take up an offer that involves moving or to stay put in your neighbourhood or city and keep looking. It is hard to separate from friends and acquaintances — hardest of all, perhaps, for your wife and children, and you should discuss any such prospect with them. However, distances in these days of motorways and inter-city expresses are not the gulf they once were; and the fact is that opportunities, especially in fields like advertising and communications in general, are often greater outside the regions that are considered fashionable and desirable.

Identifying a course of action

So, look back over the jobs you have done and decide which activities have given you the most satisfaction and which the least. Consider the role you tend to take in work and social situations; and review your leisure interests. Now draw the threads of these together and you will have an area of preferred activity and the type of role you are the most likely to play in it successfully. This can only be in generalised terms as yet; you know what you want from a job and how to evaluate jobs as they come along. Your 'needs matrix', as well as clearing your mind and helping you to get your priorities in perspective, will provide answers to these difficult questions: 'What is the minimum salary you are prepared to accept' or 'What salary level are you looking for'? 'Where would you be prepared to work?' 'Are you prepared to go abroad?' 'What will the reaction of your family be if you are away from home for up to three weeks at a time?' 'How mobile are you?' The point we want to make is this; if you have thought out the implications of these questions in advance you are better able to answer them and to answer them positively and with conviction. This will not only impress the interviewer who feels you are a man who has faced up to reality and is making the best possible use of a difficult situation and knows his own mind, but also you are no longer a hostage to fate; you are in command of your destiny.

A self-assessment test
This section, and the questions about yourself which it asks you to answer, will help you to rate yourself as objectively as a potential employer or personnel consultant might do. It will also serve to clarify some of your attitudes towards such matters as the importance you attach to things like status and money. Thus it will help you to complete application blanks and prepare yourself for those questions that are sometimes difficult to answer off the cuff in interviews.

1. Attainments
The high spots of what you have achieved so far. For simplicity we look at these from three different angles.
Academic — educational qualifications; grades.
Professional — range and depth of your job-knowledge and experience.
Leadership — whom you have led and in what circumstances you were chosen.

Academic
Highest formal exams passed (school, college/university or private study) to map academic strengths and weaknesses:
Exam ....
Subjects taken ....
Grades awarded ....
Now list your two best and two weakest subjects at each stage of your formal education. Do the same thing for any subjects you have taken by private study and for any courses you have taken.

Professional
List the principal aspects of your job as it is generally

40

practised (e.g. if you are a chief executive, this might include such matters as an acquaintance with accounting techniques, production technology, marketing, computer applications, etc.) and grade your knowledge as follows:

0 — no experience
1 — casual or second-hand experience
2 — some experience/knowledge (would need help or have to read up to perform satisfactorily)
3 — good experience in the past, but out-of-date now
4 — competent
5 — expert

Leadership
by appointment   role
School   . . . .
College/university   . . . .
Armed services   . . . .
Other organisations   . . . .
At work   . . . .
by consent or election   role
School   . . . .
College/university   . . . .
Other organisations   . . . .
At work   . . . .
Which category most applies to you?
Tend to be a leader in most situations
                    in formal situations only
                         (by appointment)
                    in informal situations only
                         (by election)
Reluctant to exercise leadership function when appointed or elected
Tend to take a 'number two' role
No leadership experience worth mentioning.

2. Basic aptitudes
We all have our own way of solving problems — the politician manipulates people, i.e. he gets somebody else to do the work for him!; the salesman talks his way through (or out of) trouble; the engineer resorts to paper and drawing board; the

craftsman to his work-bench. It is important to recognise our own basic aptitudes — or the lack of them. Rate your own basic aptitudes from the following list by awarding yourself (6) for the highest to (1) for the lowest and (—) for any you simply do not possess.

Verbal —
(a) Spoken: you follow arguments easily; can argue or negotiate persuasively and skilfully; have a large vocabulary; people listen to you.
(b) Written: you read quickly; communicate well on paper; enjoy writing reports; have a large vocabulary.

Numerical —
You are happiest when working with figures or formulae; resort to a slide-rule or use stats. whenever feasible; fill your reports with figures and argue from quantifiable 'facts'.

Practical —
(a) You resort to pencil and paper sketches/diagrams whenever you can; can think in three dimensions.
(b) You like to work with things or go down to the shop floor to work things out; prefer to tackle down-to-earth 'real' problems rather than to speculate on theoretical possibilities.

Creative —
You enjoy playing with ideas, testing hypotheses, and coming up with novel solutions (even if impractical); the 'status quo' frustrates you and you are always trying to change the system; may be inventive or artistic.

Methodical —
Everything you do is neatly set out — home, workshop, office files and drawers, etc.; you rarely make careless mistakes in calculations or grammar; have a good memory for facts and figures; are a great one for law, order and method.

People-oriented —
You are a facilitator, fixer or

co-ordinator; work through people — you marshall your resources for them to solve your problems; are good at persuading people, influencing them and working up support for or against an issue; have a way with people that tends to command their allegience.

3. Interests and hobbies

Most of us cherish the hope of pursuing some interest or other 'if only we could find the time to get around to it'; for instance writing or painting. But if in practice you have never found the leisure time to devote to your pipedream then you probably have no deep motivation to develop it further. However, if there are any hobbies or interests that you are actively involved in, put them down. They may have considerable occupational significance, particularly if they highlight talents that you are not able to employ in your job.

Interest	*Time spent per week*	*Rank order*
Helping people (e.g. voluntary social work)	. . . .	. . . .
Persuading people (e.g. local politics, lecturing)	. . . .	. . . .
Experimenting with words or ideas (e.g. writing, Open University study)	. . . .	. . . .
Scientific or mathematical	. . . .	. . . .
Developing manual or technical skills (e.g. carpentry, photography)	. . . .	. . . .
The Arts (music, painting, etc.)	. . . .	. . . .
Outdoor activities and sports	. . . .	. . . .
Collecting (antiques, etc.)	. . . .	. . . .
Others	. . . .	. . . .

4. Personality

We all have persistent personality traits which enable other people to predict how we are likely to act or react to certain 'typical' life or social situations. It is these persistent traits that you should concentrate on here. Base your conclusions on how you have in reality reacted in the past not on how you might have acted if things had been different!

In career guidance psychologists concentrate on four main traits:

- (a) sociable vs. self-contained
- (b) phlegmatic vs. excitable
- (c) tough-minded vs. sensitive
- (d) conforming vs. independent

In each of the following there are five possible reactions. Read each pair, ask yourself which reaction applies to you, and tick only those that do. When you have done this add up your scores on sides A and B and subtract one from the other to give a positive score. If the final score in any category is less than 3 this particular trait is not significant for you. Keep a note of score above 3, and finally check conclusions with a friend to avoid bias.

(a) Are you sociable or self-contained?

A	B
Lively and talkative	Quiet and subdued
Warm-hearted and sociable	Shy and self-contained
Adventurous, welcome new situations and challenges	Conservative (with a small c), dislike fresh challenge or changes
Impulsive, quickly change plans	Controlled, only change plans after thinking them through carefully
Easy-going, have many friends	Serious, a few deep friendships

If your score on A is higher than on B then you are sociable; if B is higher than A you are self-contained. If your scores balance out then this trait is not significant for you.

44

(b) Are you phlegmatic or excitable?

A	B
Patient, willing to wait	Impatient, want to do things straight away
Placid, not easily upset	Anxious, easily upset
Careful, concerned to make good	Careless, not very concerned about the impression made on others
Relaxed	Tense and restless
Slow to be roused to activity	Quickly roused to activity

Score as above. Caution: it is easy to draw moral conclusions from your answers here. The fact that you are inclined to be anxious and careless does not mean that you are necessarily irresponsible or cannot be depended upon. But it may well mean that you have to overcompensate for these tendencies and that a stressful job or situation will make heavier demands on you psychologically than it will on others.

(c) Are you tough-minded or sensitive?

A	B
Practical and realistic	Imaginative
Enjoy rough activities	Avoid rough activities
Prefer to do things yourself	Seek and welcome help from others
Appear hard and tough to others	Appear soft and gentle to others
Dislike emotion and sentiment	Welcome expressions of emotion or expressions of feelings

Score as above. Caution: in our society sensitivity is associated with femininity and toughness with masculinity and there are cultural pressures to reinforce this from infancy. In practice, the reverse is often true. The sensitive diplomat can outmanoeuvre the tough-minded soldier; and tough-minded managers often run into human-relations problems.

(d) Are you conforming or independent?

A	B
Welcome direction and advice	Resent 'interference' and advice
Submissive, go along with friends' or colleagues' suggestions	Assertive, like to get your own way
Prefer conventional and traditional ideas	Radical and welcome change and go out to achieve it for its own sake
Conscientious, keep to the rules	Prepared to break the rules if it suits your purpose
Follow the beliefs of others and accept their attitudes	Prefer to make up your own mind and disbelieve if not convinced.

Score as above.

Your personal profile

1. Attainments (from p. 40)
(a) Academic
Your highest scholastic achievement:
at school . . . .
at college/university . . . .
private study . . . .

(b) Professional
Summary from p. 41.

(c) Leadership
Most significant attainments from p. 41

2. Basic aptitudes
Tick the following as appropriate from your answers on p. 42:

Verbal	Creative
Numerical	Methodical
Practical	People-oriented

3. Interests and hobbies
Record your conclusions from p. 43.

4. Personality
Tick as appropriate and record positive scores.

sociable	self-contained
phlegmatic	excitable
tough-minded	sensitive
conforming	independent

What are you best equipped to do?

Most people are able to do quite a number of different jobs largely depending on the opportunities presented to them and on the society in which they live. The more intelligent you are and the wider your range of interests, the wider your range of choice. Nevertheless you are likely to derive a greater satisfaction from jobs which most nearly match the profile of academic attainments, aptitudes, interests, and personality which you have now built up.

Assuming that you are over 35 — or at least over 30 — many of the options open to you earlier will now have gone or be too costly to attain due to family responsibilities or lack of money. If you wish to make a change, review the alternatives in a logical way concentrating on your strengths and being aware of your weaknesses. Consider the activity, the level and the environment of the work you have done and of the possible openings to you. Try to change only one variable; to attempt more may be too heavily demanding psychologically.

Activity. This may be the time to improve your qualifications and thus specialise in an aspect of your work that especially interests you. The salesman may decide to come inside and become a buyer; the production engineer a tester or maintenance engineer; the researcher, a teacher or trainer.

Level. Broadly, you have the choice of coasting along at your present level or of climbing the ladder; to step backwards is very difficult — unless you break right away. If you wish to climb you must be very realistic when assessing your abilities. In many instances it will demand further study, perhaps higher qualifications, and make very heavy demands on your time and on you personally. By all means realise your full potential but don't overreach yourself. The solution for you may be to be a bigger fish in a smaller pond or to take a senior staff job with no departmental responsibilities.

Environment. The environment within which you have worked may, on reflection, be more important to you than the actual work you do; or vice versa. We are all familiar with the problems created by a change at the top especially after a takeover or merger. Try to match the new environment with your own personality and think hard and long before making a fundamental change.

Obviously, within the confines of this book, it would be impossible and grossly misleading to attempt to guide each individual reader towards a specific career change. What we can do, however, is to help you to match yourself with the career profiles of successful people in broad occupational areas or 'career types'. If, to a substantial extent, it does not match the job you are in, then you should seriously consider making a change by transfer to another department or activity or leaving the company for a more challenging or congenial environment. If that change would involve upsetting more than one of the three variables — work activity, level or environment — then we strongly suggest that you seek professional guidance from one of the bodies listed in chapter 7.

Career types

Executive/Decision-Making

You enjoy running things and taking policy-decisions; you are interested in broad issues and the interpretation of data prepared by others.

Academic — any subject, preferably at pass degree level as a minimum

Professional — rate 4 or 5 in at least 50% of the relevant areas of job knowledge

Leadership — tend to lead in most situations. Lots of initiative

Aptitude — verbal/numerical and people-oriented

Strongest interests — competitive activities, social

organisations
Personality — self-contained, tough-minded, independent
Jobs to consider — running an operation or part of an operation, carrying profit or other objective-attaining responsibility

Administrative
You tend to be strongest in the following:
Academic — languages, social studies or science; tend to have performed well in exams
Professional — likely to be fully qualified but not 'brilliant'
Leadership — Like responsibility, but prefer No. 2 role
Aptitude — methodical, verbal (b), or numerical
Strongest interests — working with figures, words or ideas. Outdoor, active
Personality — self-contained, phlegmatic, conforming
Jobs to consider — company secretary, local government, civil service, consultancy

Altruistic
As the word implies, you enjoy work that involves helping others, with financial gain as a secondary consideration.
Academic — languages or social studies
Professional — may have background in personnel or some other people-oriented function
Leadership — social organisations, e.g. local politics, church activities
Leisure — involves voluntary social work, e.g. marriage guidance
Aptitude — verbal or people-oriented
Strongest interest — helping people or organising; words and ideas
Personality — sociable, excitable, sensitive

Artistic
You enjoy work that involves creativity or inventiveness (by doing or appreciation).
Academic — languages, art or craft subjects
Professional — may not have bothered to qualify
Leadership — good in situations that require initiative and

49

persistence
Interests — artistic or craft skills
Aptitude — creative
Strongest interests — the arts, working with materials or tools, persuading people
Personality — self-contained, excitable, independent
Jobs to consider — setting up on one's own to fulfil the growing demand for craftsman-made, 'one-off' objects that big organisations no longer supply, e.g. cabinet-making, metalwork, restoring antiques or pictures, etc.

Literary

You like working with words, ideas and feelings.
Academic — languages or social studies
Professional — probably good professional qualifications
Leadership — unimportant
Leisure — writing and serious reading
Aptitude — verbal or creative
Strongest interests — words and ideas, the arts, persuading people
Personality — sociable, excitable, independent
Jobs to consider — technical writer, librarian, information or communication specialist (in company). Possibly writing — though, as with all the arts, you have to achieve a very high standard to earn a living!

Persuasive

You enjoy work which influences others towards a course of action. This may involve getting them to buy something or, in another sphere, bringing them together for the purposes of an organisation.
Academic — languages, the arts, or social studies
Professional — possibly no formal qualifications
Leadership — elective leadership, especially where initiative and persistence required
Leisure — will have taken part in money-raising (e.g. school or club funds), voluntary PR, or organising social events
Aptitude — people-oriented, verbal (a)
Strongest interest — words or ideas, competitive sports
Personality — sociable, tough-minded, independent

Jobs to consider — advertising, public relations, sales and marketing, fund-raising organisation consultant, personnel officer, full-time club secretary

Practical
You would enjoy a skilled job that would involve working with your hands.
Academic — practical subjects
Professional — craft or technical qualifications and training
Leadership — not important but might have been a formally appointed supervisor
Leisure — do-it-yourself, especially working with raw materials rather than ready-made kits
Aptitude — practical
Strongest interests — working with materials, the arts, helping people with practical projects
Personality — phlegmatic, sensitive, conforming
Jobs to consider — working in a laboratory in a skilled capacity, owning a garage or repair workshop; skilled building crafts or home-improvement franchise

Scientific
You have a basic curiosity and interest in how and why things happen.
Academic — scientific or mathematical subjects
Professional — academic rather than technical qualifications, possibly involving subjects pursued for their own sake rather than their possible commercial applications
Leadership — small group leadership (by election or consent)
Leisure — some private work of observation of a scientific nature
Aptitude — numerical
Strongest interests — working with tools or materials, science, music
Personality — self-contained, phlegmatic, independent
Jobs to consider — teaching at secondary or tertiary level, research and development in industry, working with computers

Technical/Technological

You enjoy work in an environment where tools and machinery are involved.

Academic — Technical, scientific or mathematical subjects

Professional — as above

Leadership — not an important factor

Leisure — enjoyment of hobbies or do-it-yourself pursuits that involve tinkering with machinery

Aptitude — practical, methodical or numerical

Strongest interests — working with tools, following developments in technology, active outdoor pursuits

Personality — phlegmatic, tough-minded, conforming

Jobs to consider — technical college teaching, the production side in industry

4   Planning a job strategy

Now is the time to bring all your business experience and expertise to bear on the most challenging and important assignment you have ever tackled — setting out to find a new executive job for yourself. The first essential is to be systematic and to operate in a planned way: as you would do if you were tackling any other kind of business operation. The stages are
1.   Set up a job file.
2.   Carry out a survey of the total market.
3.   Set your objectives against a time scale.
4.   Set an interview-getting strategy.
   This may sound very elementary to you, but it is surprising how few people get off on the right foot. The best way to make sure that you do so is to open a job file.

1. Job file
In this file you will put everything appertaining to your search — a progress chart; your self-analysis; live applications; dead applications; personal contacts.

Progress charts
On a piece of white card (card because it will be handled a lot) enter these headings — Company, Job, Salary, Location, Initial Enquiry, Application Sent, Progress. Divide the last section into six narrow vertical columns (for dates) and allow space for your written comments. Check this card daily and always keep it completely up-to-date. As jobs fall through run a thin red line through the entry.
   Behind this card keep a series of 'call reports' — that is, fuller notes for your future guidance of the names of people met at interview; and difficulties encountered such as questions which bowled you out, deficiencies pointed out, any mistakes you think you might have made and points that

were especially well received. Do a call report for every application that goes beyond the interview stage.

You will also need to keep a note of your investigations into companies. This will include extracts from reference books, newspaper cuttings, some of their current ads (job and product), any financial information you can obtain etc. (See later for some guidelines on company investigations.) Where you keep this information is a matter of choice, but as it is possible to use it more than once we suggest you keep it in the progress chart section.

Self-analysis

This section will contain everything from chapter 3. Keep your summary and objectives on the top for ease of reference together with a copy of your summary c.v. (see chapter 8). As you go along you will want to modify or expand some points so be sure to keep your 'summary and objectives' right up to date. It is probably less cumbersome to enter alterations in the section concerned even if it does look untidy!

Live applications

Number these and keep an ease of reference index at the front. As jobs fall through (sorry, one must be realistic!) delete them from the list. It is easier to keep these in date order — as your progress chart. Every communication with the prospective employer should be recorded — phone calls and the outcome of them, correspondence and a summary of your reply or a copy if typed, and finally a note of any reason that may have been offered for turning you down. Keep the original advertisement, or an introductory note, on top for ready reference.

Dead applications

As soon as applications fall through remove them to the dead section so as not to clutter the live file and if this section becomes too long open another dead file. It is worth keeping these old papers as a job may suddenly fall vacant again or a similar one arise with the same company. Also they will be useful for study if you persistently seem to fail to get beyond the interview. There may be something wrong with your letter-writing technique which a friend will be able to point out to you.

Personal contacts
Keep a list of the names of all your useful contacts together with their address and phone code. Alongside each name make a note of when you were last in contact and for what purpose. Keep these in alphabetical order as far as possible for rapid reference if one of them phones. It is worth keeping a similar note of the people you meet at interview or are in correspondence with. Some people find it easier to keep such names in an alphabetical book or on a small desk card index.

2. Surveying the market
If you have carried out the steps in the last chapter you will have a clear idea of the direction you want to go and of your priorities. At this stage it can only be in general terms; if too specific you will probably have leapt to too hasty a conclusion and may well spend too long tackling too narrow a field. Make sure that you survey the field as widely as possible and with as few pre-conceived notions as possible. Study the *Financial Times, The Economist;* examine the economic points of the C.B.I. and the Economic Intelligence Unit; read *The Director, Management Today* and your own professional press; talk to friends 'in the know'. You will quickly begin to see how the land lies and gain a shrewd idea of the state of the employment market, of salary levels, of industries and firms on the rise and those in decline. You will also soon get a feel of technological developments and will draw conclusions on likely future trends in the shorter term. The more informed opinion you can obtain the better. Undoubtedly you will need to 'polish your crystal ball' if you want to see very far ahead but on the whole things move slowly and the 5-10 year trend is discernible. At interviews later you will be able constantly to refine your views and check your conclusions—which will have the added advantage of impressing your interviewer with the depth of your knowledge.

The kind of broad trend you might think about and of

which you can build up a picture by reading and discussion is, for example: how is the U.K.'s entry into the Common Market affecting the size and shape of British industries and commerce and what job opportunities will there be? The pattern of the last ten years on the continent is a fairly reliable guide.

Another way of getting some ideas of future developments is to look at what is happening in the U.S.A. — it often presages the pattern in Britain as was the case, for instance, with supermarkets.

On the other hand, you may be thinking of opportunities in developing countries. Here the process is reversed — they are generally behind the U.K. by at least the same margin as the U.S.A. is ahead. Many of them work on 5-10 year plans with the help of organisations such as the I.L.O. and welcome assistance from foreign experts, either as advisers or as short-term executive manpower to get their industry and commerce going and to train nationals for succession. Often skills which are obsolescent in the U.K. are in demand elsewhere — for instance, in industries employing labour-intensive production methods.

In Britain, to give another example, those who foresaw the growth of the I.T.B.s have done well. This led to an unprecedented boom for the entry of training experts to the staff of the I.T.B.s for those with senior administrative experience; to staff consultancies, training colleges, and the I.T.B.s at the professional level for men with training expertise; and within companies themselves at two levels — for experienced senior managers who understand training and can help sell it to the company's own management, and at the application end for men with practical training experience. Both of the latter have been in considerable demand; conservative boards are unlikely to take advice from a young graduate 'expert' but the man with Board experience can ease the path of the latter and himself gain some insight into this, an area with which he may not be entirely familiar.

Will not legislation in the industrial relations field give comparable openings for men with some experience of this activity at factory level? There are plenty of other points in the areas of production, marketing and technology.

Another valuable source of information is the job advertisements themselves — not only those in your own area of expertise but in general. It is said that the advertisements of the selection consultants are read avidly in top financial circles because these so often presage other developments or are the first indications that the outside world has of important changes at the top. So it will pay you to see which companies are recruiting and which are not. In some cases the jobs advertised will clearly be replacements but others will follow a typical development pattern; viz. investment in research is reflected within a year in design and development; this in turn leads to a build up in production; which in turn leads to growth in the sales force. Admittedly, this is on a fairly long time scale but by discerning such a trend you can see which firms are going ahead and where vacancies are likely to arise and in which functions. Another thing to watch is the salary and man specifications. They must be studied together. If certain skills are in short supply then man specifications are loosened (i.e. men with poorer qualifications and less experience are accepted) and salaries raised to attract new people to the industry. The M.S.L. Index, published quarterly and usually commented on in the press in some detail, gives moving totals of demand by function together with a commentary on the state of the market. This is done by a systematic analysis of all advertisements for posts carrying a certain minimum salary of seniority. By comparing one month with another, patterns can easily be discerned. From this you can soon see which categories are in demand, which in recession, salary levels, the type of people sought, age bands, and where most jobs are advertised at the salary levels you are interested in.

So to sum up you will now know

(a) the broad economic trends;
(b) trends in technology;
(c) the overall state of the job market;
(d) the state of development or retrenchment in individual firms;
(e) the demand position in your own function or area of interest.

You are in a position, therefore, to go back to your career

aims and to match these to areas of opportunity in the market. You can decide not only in which direction to launch yourself but also you will have a pretty shrewd idea of the comparative difficulty of finding a suitable vacancy and whether or not to modify your 'asking price'.

3. Setting your objectives

As you will know the more advanced managements don't muddle along in the pious hope of increasing profit each year (or maintaining dividends); they plan ahead and set themselves quantified objectives and then ensure that the organisation is right and the people well motivated to achieve these objectives within a given time scale. In your case the longer term objective is to get a job that will satisfy as many of your needs as possible; and the shorter term aim is to get interviews. The first fact you have to face is that the higher up the organisation you have been, the higher your salary, and the greater your age, the longer it will take you to get a job. That is why senior executives are given larger golden handshakes. Many factors affect this. The main ones are:

(a) It scarcely matters how expert you are in your own field or how well known, the hard fact is that there will be few vacancies at any one time for men like you.

(b) The job-filling process at senior levels is a slow one. The specialist selection consultants reckon on six weeks from initial briefing to making an offer as the very minimum. With overseas appointments six months or more is quite common; 'official' appointments will be somewhere in-between. It is extremely unlikely that you will walk straight into a job — though we hope you will — and if you receive a firm offer in the early days you should consider very carefully before turning it down and playing hard to get — because you will be in the lucky top 5%.

The time scale of probability

As a rule of thumb the very minimum time (for that lucky 5%) will be one month. Add to this the period of notice you have to give if you are already in employment; if you have been warned of impending redundancy you may be released earlier (unless a company is being kept going until the last possible moment in which case you may be offered a premium or the size of your handshake may depend on your staying until the bitter end). Add to this another month for each five years over 35 and another month for each £1,000 above £3,500 p.a. So the 39 year old aiming at £4,500+ (essential minimum) is likely to take at least three months; the 46 year old aiming at £6,000+ — seven months; the 52 year old £10,000 p.a. man — well over 12 months. If you are unlucky or become redundant at a time when the recruitment market is slack (especially June-August; November-December) it may well take even longer. So if you decide to go into business on your own account by investing your 'golden handshake' in a pub or a chain of holiday cottages the sooner you get started the better. Keep this time scale of probability firmly in mind (write it beneath your aims and objectives inside your job file; it will reassure you when you receive the 20th or 200th refusal). On the other hand don't let it lull you into a sense of false security. It doesn't mean that in six months' time the right job will turn up; it means that if you market yourself effectively with sustained effort within six months the probability is that you will have found a suitable appointment.

How long can you afford to wait?
This is the second critical parameter to take into account. If you are in employment this is no problem; if not you may be forced to take some early, drastic action.
(a) If you limit your area of choice too strictly (so as not to upset the children's schooling) this will probably delay things even more.
(b) You must market yourself correctly and at the right price. It will be better to drop that extra £500 right from the start rather than stick out for the extra. After all £500 is only one month's salary at £6,000 p.a. and the capital you will spend during the month that you are out of work represents many months of hard saving. The hard and apparently unfair fact is that the longer you are out of work the more difficult it will be to persuade an employer that there is nothing wrong with you! Ask any

selection consultant; and wouldn't you yourself have said the same in the past? Unless you have vast financial resources or are in a job it is not advisable to play hard to get.

Naming your price

Equally it means don't underprice yourself unrealistically. The £5,000 p.a. man who is prepared to accept a senior lecturer's salary of £3,750 is one thing; but to apply for a job in his old function at £3,750 and with a much lower status is quite another. 'Why is this man prepared to drop so much? He must be desperate (and by implication useless)' – 'I know he says he is quite prepared to take a drop but how long will he stay once the market improves?' – 'Oh yes he's well qualified all right; too well qualified to be satisfied with this job – (aside) I'd have to watch out for my job if he were appointed'. And so on. You've probably heard this sort of thing said.

So how do you fix your price? This will depend on several factors:
(a) whether or not you are in employment;
(b) whether you wish to stay in the same activity or function;
(c) whether the type of job you are now going for has an entirely different salary structure.

It could well be that you would quote a different price to different employers. If it's a choice between an inherent risk in a new consultancy, a secure post in government, and a lectureship (with the expectation of additional income from freelance consultancy) you could well be prepared to accept £6,000, £4,000, and £3,750, respectively as it is possible to adjust your life accordingly. To get a feel of current salaries find out your current salary scale; study the job advertisements in the press; and look out for commentaries on salary levels by such firms as Hay-M.S.L. and A.I.C. (but be wary of those based on what candidates would like as they are always on the high side). Depending on the strength of your own position draw up your own upper, median and lower quartiles. If you are in a job and are prepared to go to a competitor aim for the upper quartile (he will expect to pay it); or a median salary if you are aiming for a promotion; or if you are changing completely aim for the lower quartile. If you are redundant and can afford to wait, aim for the median but don't be too rigid about it. If you are close to the dole fix yourself at the lower quartile 'bargain' price — after all you are unlikely to stay at the bottom for long if you are any good. When an employer decides he wants you he may well offer you a little more even on a fixed scale; this is certainly so with teaching and Civil Service appointments — providing that you justify it, of course. If you decide on a complete change then you will have to take the rate for the job. The ex-serviceman has to accept that he will have to start at the bottom and prove himself in civilian employment and leave it to his maturity and application to rise more rapidly than most. I think that this is accepted by ex-servicemen today but it was not always so and I suspect that many redundant executives find it hard to accept.

4. An interview-getting strategy

By now you have decided on the type of job you are aiming for, you have fixed a time scale and you have set an offer price and are ready for the launch.

You need not feel, however, that you are now entirely on your own; there are other forces you can deploy to your advantage at each stage of your job-getting campaign. Timing will depend on your judgement and the strength of your need (see chapter 7 — Consultancies, agencies and others who can help you). Likewise, the length of time between each phase of your search will depend on the 'time scale of necessity'.

Phase 1. The publicity, test marketing phase

A new product will not sell until it is known to be on offer. So the first essential step is to make sure that the people who are most likely to be able to help you are aware that you are on the market and what your preferences are. This will include your personal contacts, executive search and selection consultancies. If you are in a job this can present problems. You will need to be very discreet as there have been cases of executives being sacked for disloyalty when it has been discovered that they are 'looking around'. The higher up the ladder you are the more important discretion becomes because of possible effects on the stock market. How you declare your availability will depend on your status, salary level, occupation, and the attitude of your present employer.

Phase 2. Study the ads
At all levels this will follow closely on phase 1. It is vital that you do not let up your efforts until you have a firm, confirmed offer in your hand. This is the ad watching stage. To save you looking at every publication and reading every ad there are certain useful guidelines. Few jobs over £3,000 a year appear in the local press. Few jobs over £3,500 will appear in the regional press *alone*. Most managerial jobs appear in the quality daily and weekend press — *The Sunday* and *The Daily Telegraph, The Sunday Times, The Observer, The Times* and *The Guardian.* The *Daily Express* and the *Daily Mail* occasionally carry professional and managerial jobs though usually at the lower salary level. At this stage we suggest that you go to your local library and scan all these for at least a week to get a feel of the market you are particularly interested in and to mark which days are the most popular for advertising (traditionally Monday and Saturday are poor days). Then you can pick out the most promising dailies and Sundays and study them *every* day. If you have capital to invest then you should add the *F. T.* to your list.

The evening papers are also mostly of use only at the under £3,000 level. Another rule of thumb is to read only your own professional column and the management and executive column in lineage and then study the display columns (and some of these are classified too). There are separate pages for public and official appointments. The consultancy firms usually advertise on set days — Wednesday, Thursday and Friday being the most popular.

The next must is your own professional journals. These vary enormously but in, for example, medicine, law and architecture some 90% of all job ads for the professions are contained in one or two professional journals. In personnel management some 60% appear only in the official journal. At times of mounting executive redundancy companies will tend to place the bulk of their advertising for jobs in the main professional journals, thus saving considerable sums. We suggest that you start by looking through back numbers — remember it can take three months to fill a job and the application list is usually kept open until the last moment (except with official appointments). Follow up urgently anything that interests you, preferably by phone. At this stage it will pay you to be fairly selective. Go for the jobs you really want and apply to them first and leave the others to one side for a week or two. Cut out the ads and mount them in your job file and record action taken.

Phase 3. The cold canvass
If phases 1 and 2 are patently not producing results, or if a shortage of funds demands more drastic action, you should start thinking in terms of the cold canvass. Choose your firms carefully, or else you will end up with a large duplicating and postage bill and find yourself sending out 1,000 letters! The most useful way to set about it is

1. Study the information provided in the standard works of reference which are listed in Appendix D. These provide a wealth of data on who manufactures what and where, on company policies and plans and, in some cases, on future developments.
2. Read the financial and business press regularly. It will give you an up-to-the-minute picture of which firms are expanding and in what directions — both in terms of activities and geographically. Try to spot their needs for someone like yourself *before* they advertise. This is not as difficult as it might sound. For example, a new factory will require executive staff to man it or to replace others who are withdrawn from elsewhere in the company; a merger/takeover may well mean openings for men with big company experience or men to replace an ageing and ailing management team; the introduction of a new product; or the receipt of a very large order; or the introduction of a computer will all probably call for additional staff some at relatively senior levels; the appointment of Mr. X may mean a reshuffle of the entire management team and the introduction of a new

style of management; and so on. Admittedly this is more useful at the junior-middle management levels (top management will have been decided in advance) but it is not always so. Very frequently companies fail to realise the scope for a good man or the contribution he could make until they are confronted with one who can spell out the details for them and they have physically seen him. Some guidance on writing 'on spec' letters is given in Appendix A. But you have to face the fact that although a far-sighted management will make the job to fit the man, relatively few come into this category — so be prepared for a vast number of rejections!

Registers and placement agencies

A list of such agencies — they are not very many — is given in chapter 7. Placement agencies will see you, evaluate you, give advice and place your name on their register if they think they can help you. It must, however, be remembered that these people are in business to fill jobs — not to offer careers counselling as such — and they will only interview you if they think there is a strong chance of placing you in a specific job. They offer no miracles or instant solutions, as the people who run them will readily admit. If you are outstandingly good in your field, the executive placement agencies can be very useful — but then you may not have much trouble anyway. In short, they are one of the many tools at your disposal.

Advertising your availability

Should you advertise yourself? On the whole, the opinion is that, as far as the national press is concerned, this is highly unlikely to produce results, unless you have capital to invest or would like to buy a directorship in a small firm. In that case you should clearly specify what you want and what you have to offer, for example

Return on £30,000 investment and energetic participation sought by experienced retail store executive. Reply to Box No. 1234, *Daily Telegraph*.

The box number is a good idea, because it avoids calls at your home from the undesirable characters who unfortunately tend to be attracted by the notion of someone with money to invest.

The professional press is well worth using, if you have a specific qualification or skill that you can offer, for example

> Distribution problems? Experienced physical distribution manager, who has controlled both manual and automated systems for leading motor parts manufacturer available now. Box. No. 5678, *Commercial Motor.*

Advertising in professional or specialist journals is a lot cheaper than in national newspapers, and you can pick with some precision the potential employers you are trying to reach. You may therefore find it advantageous to go for display rather than line advertising. This is more eye-catching and in some papers you can actually specify the position you want your advertisement to appear on the page.

A job strategy check list for top, middle and junior management

Top management
Provided that you stay in your present function the personal contact at the club, by private letter (sent to a home address) or phone call (again from home) will soon get the ball rolling under control. A word with your financial advisers may well bear fruit — they may be able to put you in touch with company chairmen who need someone with your expertise but who for commercial reasons daren't say so openly until the deal is completed.

If it can be made public a carefully worded press announcement, which contains some specific reference to what you have done, issued through your P.R. advisers may help enormously, e.g. 'One of the casualties from the forthcoming merger between x and y will be John Smith the Marketing Director of y and the man largely responsible for its growth from sales of £300,000 four years ago to the forecast £2.5m. this year. I understand that he has already been offered several alternatives in the new organisation but feels that he would rather head up the function in a new and developing company. As a result of the merger company x's well known market development procedures will be introduced throughout the group giving little scope for an ideas man like John Smith. The changeover is not likely to be fully effective until the new year.' This type of announcement will lead to many offers and your name will be noted by all the executive search consultants (head hunters!). Any reputable management selection consultancy should also be approached. Some will see you; others will want particulars to keep on file; others will advise you to watch their advertisement columns — but they will all be interested to hear from you. A short note setting out what you are looking for accompanied by a well set-out curriculum vitae will be quite sufficient and avoid filling out application blanks unnecessarily at this stage.

Middle Management

If you are in the £3,500-£6,000 bracket you are probably not sufficiently well known to adopt the P.R. release aproach and will need to use your personal contacts in a different way. To be brutal, it is less likely that you will be on christian name terms with company chairmen and the company's City advisers. On the other hand you may well have met a number of influential people who may be in a position to help you. Unless you are likely to command a salary in excess of £6,000 p.a. the executive search consultants are not likely to be interested in you, but the management selection firms will be very glad to know you! If during the last three years you have met one of these consultants by all means contact him (by appointment so that he can look up your records). He may well be prepared to give you half an hour's free advice and perhaps circulate your papers among his colleagues. On the whole these companies do not keep lists of potential candidates and will advise you to 'watch their columns' — but they are always glad to hear from a man with a good record. I would not advocate 'cold canvass' or employing executive placement consultants (if you have to pay a fee) at this stage unless you wish to make a very radical change in your career direction primarily because of the expense and the sheer tedium of preparing and sending out literally hundreds of cold canvass letters, the vast majority of which will be futile — unless you are in a very small profession such as an actuary. Marketing personnel and salesmen seem to like the cold canvass but they usually choose the firms they select with considerable care because this method is regarded with scepticism by the recipients. (These men are usually the hardest hit by a recession.)

Junior management/professional men

Once again the personal contact may be useful. The executive search firm will not be interested and the selection consultants in general will only tell you to watch their columns. However, the specialist selection firms may well be able to help you — the computer, accountancy, marketing, advertising, personnel specialists spring to mind. This apart, advertising yourself is unlikely to be very useful as the hard fact is that you are unlikely to be well known or in especially short supply. The principal exception could be if you are known in your field as a writer or lecturer or are in the public eye. Here again, though, you will be able most probably to use personal contacts.

A final word

You will go through periods when you are full of optimism — and all five jobs fall through — and others of profound despair when nothing seems to turn up for weeks. It is absolutely vital for your own morale and for your ultimate success that you maintain the pressure all the time. Don't delay moving on to the next phase unnecessarily; maintain your daily study of the press; keep up your contacts and above all don't give up.

5   Making the most of your contacts

Whenever opinions are canvassed about the most effective method of getting a job, personal contacts and introductions come up as the answer. Apart from internal promotion more people get jobs through direct or indirect recommendations and leads from friends, acquaintances and colleagues than by any other means. This fact is borne out in a recent B.I.M. report *Selecting Managers* which shows that only about 50% of executive jobs are ever advertised openly. The majority are either filled by promotion or through personal contact. It is well known that when a new company chairman is sought the first people to be approached are the merchant banks; for a company secretary — city solicitors; for financial heads — the companies' auditors.

This is not because the old boy network is more rampant in Britain than anywhere else, but simply because interviewing is still a fairly inexact science in terms of guaranteeing that square pegs will be placed in square holes. Even the expert interviewer, when he has deployed all his skills, will still be left with a strong element of hunch. It is then, and if all other things are more or less equal between the last two candidates, that the opinion of a third party about a man, framed in a way that is relevant to his capacity to do the job in question, can be a clincher. If this is true for the expert, it is even more the case where the interview is being conducted by a manager who has no special knowledge or experience of interviewing techniques and who has either been landed with the job of finding someone to fill a vacancy, or who has to make a final decision between various candidates put forward by his personnel department or consultants. Indeed in smaller firms, a manager often decides to take a man who comes to him with a strong recommendation from a reliable source, rather than go through the rigmarole of advertising, interviewing, and eventually taking a chance on someone who is, after all that, still an unknown quantity. But even if you do not know many people whose word will carry weight with a potential employer, your friends and acquaintances can act as an intelligence service for job leads, as well as helping you to advertise your availability by word of mouth.

But before you jump to the conclusion of the well-known saying, 'It isn't what you know, but who you know' (which is anyway a good deal less than a half-truth) let us hasten to add that making the most of your contacts requires just as much thought, planning and skill as any other aspect of your job search. Indiscriminate appeals for help, along the lines of 'let me know if you hear of anything', are shots in the dark: you might strike something out there, but you are far more likely to do so if you can see your target, know where to hit it and what adjustment you have to make to your sights. In other words, you should sit down and analyse exactly *who* can help you, *how* they can help you and *what* sort of information they need to do this effectively.

In the first place you have to be clear about where the limits of your contacts' ability to help you lie in relation to your needs and qualifications. For instance, your closest friend may be the financial director of a major public company, but you know that most of the people he mixes with in a business capacity are financial people. Therefore, if you are a production man, asking him to let you know if something comes up is unlikely to take you much further. You have to think of the help he can practicably give you — it may be a recommendation, or it may be information about a planned expansion in a company he knows of — and brief him in those terms. If you look at the situation in this way you will find that the range of contacts who can help you is wider than you had imagined. They need not be people who can actually give you a job or even influential men whose recommendation will pull weight with an interviewer. Anybody who can give you a job lead that you can work on is worth bearing in mind. So you should draw up for your job file a list of all the relevant contacts you have, noting what sort of work they do, how senior they are and whether they know you in a social or a business capacity. These factors will determine what they are likely to be able to do for you.

Business acquaintances

Most people will want to start among their immediate business acquaintances and for a man in mid-career these will often be personal friends as well. If you have been fortunate enough to have been in a job that involves a lot of contact with your counterparts in other companies you obviously start off with a big advantage over those whose opportunities in this respect have been more limited, or who find it more difficult to make friends. But even if your circle is limited to colleagues in your own company do not hesitate to approach them — remember they may have outside contacts, even if you do not. (At the same time, if you are still employed, and 'just looking' you should be very careful to talk only to people you can trust absolutely not to gossip around the office, since this can sometimes provide an excuse for asking you to leave.) Do not forget, either, to add to your list former colleagues, superiors, or even subordinates who know your work and who have moved on to other firms — even if your contact with them since then has only been intermittent.

You may wind up with a list of fifty people, or it may be only five. But whatever the number it is not enough to phone and say casually that you are thinking of moving from your present position, or that you have left your company and that you would be glad if they would let you know if they hear of anything. An approach which is casual (maybe for reasons of pride) will invite an equal lack of urgency in the way they will set about helping you. Apart from that it does not give your contact enough information. You may think he knows all about you — but does he? He knows that you are an intelligent, well-informed sort of chap who has held a responsible job, who is good company over a dinner table and who maybe plays a useful game of golf. But what does he know of your performance as an executive? It is that which counts.

Put yourself, for a moment, in the position of your friend or acquaintance. He knows you are looking for a job and that you appear to have been, say, an experienced and successful managing director. So now he calls up a contact of his own, whom he knows to be looking for a chief executive. If that contact is at all alert and competent he will want to know what your qualifications are, what you have achieved, what sort of experience you have had and probably why you left or want to leave your last job. If your acquaintance is unable to answer these questions, his contact will respect him as someone who is trying to do a friend a favour, but the effect of his approach on your own chances is likely to be minimal. If, however, your acquaintance can ring his contact and say that he thinks he might have just the man he is looking for, and is in a position to tell him why, you are going to start off with a big advantage over those applicants who have no evidence to back up the facts in the c.v.

So instead of just calling your acquaintance up take the trouble to go and see him or suggest a meeting over lunch or a drink. You will want to keep things on the informal footing of a business meeting between equals — for that is what it is — but that does not mean to say you should not be getting down to brass tacks. Give him as much specific information as possible — the kind of information you would want about an executive who was being recommended to you; but do not ask him for a job, even if you have reason to believe he might have an opening for you. He knows you are looking for one. You have placed the facts about yourself at his disposal. Let the initiative come from him. You have asked for a meeting, not a job interview, and a request of that kind, if he is unprepared for it, might be embarassing for both parties. In any case your contact will usually want to discuss the matter with his colleagues before talking to you in more detail.

But even if your acquaintance is unable to come up, then and there, with a concrete suggestion of whom you might approach, the mere fact that you have given him some hard information about yourself, your qualifications and your achievements will enable him to start thinking meaningfully about possible job leads. When he does come up with a suggestion — now or later — that you approach some firm or other which he thinks might be looking for someone of your calibre, don't just note the name of the company; get as much information out of him as you can. Find out about the problems and opportunities they present, what qualifications you have that might be of particular interest to them, what the gossip is about them, whether your contact can suggest any specific person you should write to, and whether he knows any third party who can give you further information of use in an interview.

Assuming your contacts are just that — not close friends — it is a good idea to send them an informal note of thanks after you have spoken to them. Apart from the fact that such courtesies are always appreciated — even where they are not expected — it serves a useful purpose in giving your acquaintance a record of your address and the telephone number at which you can be reached. You can also, of course, put down any further points which you might have forgotten to bring up when you met.

Having sown the seeds, the awkward questions arise of when and how often you check to see whether they are taking root. Too frequent calls can become an embarassment to caller and recipient alike; equally, if you make no attempt to follow up your original enquiry, this might be taken as a sign that you have lost interest. The best plan is to make a note in your job file, showing when you spoke to your contact, what suggestions he made and what you did about them. Let about a month elapse before reaching him again and telling him what has happened. From the nature of his response, and his general manner, you should be able to get a good idea of whether it is worth keeping in touch with him, or whether it is best to let the matter drop quietly.

Top level contacts

Your circle of contacts may embrace some people who are 'big names' — major business leaders, government ministers and such-like. An endorsement or recommendation from someone at this level can obviously be invaluable, but in general terms it should be appropriate to the calibre of job you are seeking. If you are in middle management a recommendation from a nationally known chairman of a large company may seem somewhat inappropriate in terms of the job you are after, unless you can show that he knows you in a business, rather than a social capacity — as might be the case, for instance, if you are both on the committee of some public or professional body. An endorsement from someone with whom you make up the occasional four at golf is better than nothing, of course, but it is not likely to produce much information about your managerial abilities; and it is obviously a mistake to ask a man for that kind of recommendation if he is only in a position to talk about your social or athletic gifts.

Unless you happen to know the man concerned quite well, it is generally best to make your initial approach in writing rather than by telephone as your call will first be routed through, and may probably be garbled by secretaries and personal assistants. Your letter should be brief; don't go into details. Here is an example of the kind of note that, at this stage, should be quite sufficient.

Dear Sir Leonard,

You may remember that, as export director of John Wilson Ltd, I served with you on the organising committee of the British week in Stuttgart. I have since then decided to leave Wilson's, and I wonder whether I could take up a few minutes of your time to get the benefit of your advice on any opportunities that might be open to a man with my kind of experience in export in general and in the textile business in particular.

May I phone your secretary in a few days to find out a time that will be convenient to you?

Short, to the point, containing a reminder of the circumstances under which you met (important people, like the rest of us, may not immediately connect names with faces or events), positive without being aggressive and implying an understanding that your visit will not take up too much of his time — such a letter should produce a response; and if a date and place is suggested in writing you should, of course, confirm that you will be there.

Handling the meeting

You have promised not to take up more than a few minutes of your distinguished acquaintance's time. This might mean fifteen minutes or half an hour. From the atmosphere, from the pace of the questions and answers you will probably get the feeling of how long you have to put over your message. There might even be a hint at the beginning that he is pressed for time. But if there is to be any extension of the meeting let it be at his prompting, not because you've failed to think clearly about what you want to put across. Be brief and specific. You are looking for a new job. Tell him so and tell him why. The why's should be positive: you feel you need a change, more responsibility, a more responsive climate for your ideas — or simply that you feel you are worth more than your present firm is prepared to pay you. Do not — and this cannot be stressed too strongly — run down your present employers or air any grievances that you think you might have. If they are in a mess or having problems the chances are — at least with a big company — that this fact is well known. Your interviewer will respect you all the more if you do not raise the matter.

However, you have come here for a purpose, the same as that with which you have approached your other acquaintances — to outline what qualifications, experience and achievements you have to offer and, in the light of these, to get ideas on openings, or potential openings, for them: names of companies, names of individuals and inside information on special situations in which your talents would be of value to a potential employer. Unless you have been working at the very highest levels yourself, however, your acquaintance is less likely to come up with anything on specific job situations. It is more probable that he will suggest names of people you might get in touch with. Where this is the case it is perfectly reasonable to ask him to give you an introduction by telephone or letter; indeed the most valuable result of your visit might well be that it will open doors that would otherwise be difficult to enter. Leave it at that, though; don't ask him to 'put in a word for you', or anything like that. It is enough, in the first instance, that a very highly placed individual is suggesting someone he knows that you might be worth talking to. V.I.P.'s do not waste each other's time by suggesting that they interview a nonentity.

References and recommendations

Just as your request for help should be linked as far as possible to the specific form that help might take, so references and recommendations should be thought of in the context of a specific job situation. It is a good plan to tell your referees as much as you can about the job you have applied for — send them a copy of the advertisement or job specification if you can — and tell them why you are interested in this particular appointment. Writing references or answering discreet telephone calls is an onerous chore so do all you can to ensure that each referee is well primed by sending a c.v.

Character references should be approached with caution. Open references are virtually worthless but one that can attest your honesty in handling the Club's funds or your standing in your local community can set at rest the fear in an employer's mind as to integrity, especially if you are about to be given a much freer hand in your new job.

Choose your referees with a specific job in mind, do not use the same ones over and over again. Some will carry more weight in one type of job, some in another.

Always tell your referees that you have quoted their name for a specific appointment even if they have given permission to use their name in principle — and let them know the outcome with a polite note of thanks for their help, not only as a courtesy but as an indication that they should now cease their efforts on your behalf in this particular situation.

The type of people you should consider among your contacts include:

Former bosses

Former subordinates

Senior executives you know well in almost any company

Clients

Customers

Contacts made at seminars, trade fairs and at official company functions

The company's auditors, solicitors, brokers and bankers

Personal friends

A letter asking a friend for a reference might run something like this:

Dear John,

You will remember that you very kindly offered to allow me to use your name as a referee when the occasion should present itself. May I now take you up on this?

I have been shortlisted for a job as head of the division for management development and training services for the Machine Manufacturers' Association, and they have asked me to provide a personal reference.

I am sending you a copy of the advertisement that I originally answered and which sets out the job specification. I imagine the most helpful kind of reference you could give me would be one that would spell out how successful, from your knowledge of my career, you feel I would be in handling the job they have outlined.

Many thanks for your help.

6   Answering job advertisments effectively

You have now begun to put out feelers and have contacted those people who might be in a position to help you directly or indirectly. Now you are moving to phase 2 and about to scan the national press, specialist press and journals in your own field for suitable vacancies. You still have a reasonable amount of time and should use it to the full. This means applying for *every* job in your target area which meets your salary requirements. Do not half-heartedly pick at this task as some people do, resentful of the fact that they are having to look for a job; you cannot afford to let *any* opportunity pass at this stage. Apply yourself purposefully and systematically every day and make sure that every application is your best effort. Don't hesitate to approach employer B while you are on employer A's short-list. If you end up with two jobs to choose from, so much the better. In most cases it is going to take you quite a time to find the right post and the more you try for, the greater the probability that you will succeed sooner rather than later — provided that you apply for suitable jobs, of course.

Begin by scanning the publication rapidly and mark any advertisements of interest. Then go back and re-read them cutting out those you decide to follow up. It is essential that you are realistic about this. If you don't meet at least two-thirds of the specification you will be wasting your time and giving yourself needless frustration.

As a broad generalisation job advertisements are now better written — especially those of the consulting firms which specialise in recruitment advertising — but many placed by well-established, specialist agencies still leave much to be desired. To be charitable this is partly the fault of the media owners who do not lay down sufficiently high standards so that the advertiser who insists on his copy being printed, however inadequate it may be, invariably gets away with it. The headline, sub-head and lead-in should show clearly to whom the advertisement is addressed and reflect the U.S.P.s (unique selling points) or excitement of the job. Succeeding paragraphs should give sufficient information for the right men to read between the lines and get a feel of the size and measure of the job and its responsibilities; this should be in the context of the company — location, activity, size, turnover or other critical data; an outline of the candidate — by age, qualifications, and experience and outlook; the principal terms of contract — salary, main fringe benefits, holidays; and finally the action required. The typical consultants' advertisement will give all of this in under 150 words.

In practice, many employers describe jobs in terms of the qualities they would like to see in candidates with a generous element of wishful thinking. Highly critical factors such as salary, location, principal accountabilities are omitted (they might give too much away!) or so little is said that the whole thing is quite meaningless. So caveat emptor! If the advertisement is specific you have few problems. Either this job is for you or it isn't; either you fit the candidate specification or you don't. In other words, the advertisement does the preliminary sifting for both employer and candidate. Many research studies have been published telling employers what candidates look for in job advertisements but few employers seem to take much notice!

So if the advertisement lacks critical information — and probably 75% do! — you have to learn to interpret them (rather like those of house agents). One could produce a glossary of terms —

'well-established company' — old-fashioned, well-meaning but out of date.

'progressive' — just beginning to see the light of day and feeling their way slowly.

'dynamic' — hard driving; probably U.S. owned and strongly marketing oriented, etc.

Beware the long list of desired personal qualities — the advertiser hasn't a clue what he wants, and hasn't thought out the job — he just has a hazy idea of the sort of person he wants. As this is likely to be an idealised portrait of himself

25 years ago ... you learn quite a lot about the employer! Absence of salary invariable means they don't know how much to pay — and want to get away with as little as they can. (They will know how much *not* to pay — as you will find out!) Or it could be that they lack a coherent salary policy; or have a paternalistic policy; or they fear the unions or ... they are just bad payers! 'Salary commensurate with qualifications and experience' (usually inadequately described if at all) almost invariably means poor salary. A number, however, give broad guidance which is quite acceptable provided that it is not too vague: the salary band — 'candidates earning less than £4,000 are unlikely to have had sufficient responsibility'; 'starting salary will be up to £5,000 but could be more for the exceptional man'; 'salary will be negotiable around £6,000 (i.e. £5,750-£6,750)' — is adequate for you to know whether or not you are in the target area. Often salary is the most important clue as to the seniority of the job or how management regard a particular function. You can see two jobs advertised in almost identical terms; for one the salary is over £6,000 for the other £4,000.

The style of the advertisement — wording, lettering, general appearance — will invariably reflect the image of the company as an employer as well as a commercial entity — even if the advertisement has been set by the medium's own type-setters. Flamboyant and racy = marketing oriented; stilted, full of clichés = formal, rather inward looking; use of 'in' words like 'accountability', 'objectives' = up-to-date management (but possibly only just so and the consultants haven't yet left). From its wording you can learn the style of management, its attitude towards its staff, its orientation (money, people, production or sales) and from your experience you can fill in the details with a fair degree of accuracy. It is important to weigh every word in the advertisement or you could miss the fact that they need an acceptable professional to bring them up to date or a steady administrator to stabilise the organisation after a period of rapid growth but for commercial reasons dare not say so openly.

In choosing which advertisements to reply to select the most promising (probably those with salary, location and an outline of duties) and reply to them first. Speed is critical. Don't leave it several days before you reply — 48 hours is the norm. Employers expect to receive the best applicants among the first or second batch and may call these people for interview without waiting for the others to come in. So the longer you leave it the smaller your chances of an interview — even if you are well qualified. So leave to last those in which you are only marginally interested. If you are outside the specification make sure that you give a very good reason for applying. As a rule of thumb five years outside the age bracket either way is acceptable unless the advertiser has been very categorical i.e. 'candidates must be under 45'; and about £500 either side of the fixed salary will be considered by even the most rigid employers unless a salary band has been quoted. The advertiser's specifications are guidelines but don't make a fool of yourself and stray too far outside these parameters — it only leads to frustration and a waste of valuable time. Also don't try to read too much into the advertisement. Study it soberly; if there was any really attractive facet it would probably have been mentioned. Study how the employer sees the job and how he describes it and try to interpret this from your own experience and *then* project yourself into the incumbent's chair.

The initial reply
Before dashing off your application re-read each advertisement very carefully — especially the part which says how candidates should apply. The danger is that when you have replied to lots of advertisements you become careless and confused and so fall into serious errors. The initial reply is the most important one of all. If you are in doubt as to what is required play safe and send a brief covering letter with a well-prepared general curriculum vitae (c.v.). This should be two pages long at most and must set out clearly the principal facts about yourself (see chapter 8). Keep the covering letter to the point.

Dear Sir,

I am most interested in your advertisement 'Man to manage new £5M factory' which I read in today's Daily Telegraph. As you will see from the c.v. which I enclose, I have had seven years' experience managing a comparable plant at which the techniques used were probably very similar to those you will employ. Prior to that I had ten years' experience in the design/development and production engineering departments. I am now looking for the opportunity to help build up a new manufacturing unit with a forward looking management team.

I could attend for interview at almost any time with about three days' notice.

Yours truly,

Your ref. DT/35. John Smith

If the advertiser invites you to write for an application form do just that. Don't bury him in sheaves of references and work samples!

Dear Sir,
Marketing Director — ref. ST/125.

Will you please send me further information and an application form for the above post advertised in today's Sunday Telegraph.

Yours truly,
John Smith.

Even if you send a full c.v. it is highly probable that you will simply be asked to fill in an application form (hopefully with apologies) as many personnel men like to have all applications in a standard form to facilitate selection or they may use a special type of form.

Sometimes, when there is likely to be an exceptionally heavy response employers make it harder to apply. 'Please state briefly how you meet each of the requirements' or 'in your reply indicate what particular contribution you would be able to make'. These need to be thought out carefully and drafted so leave them till last unless you are especially interested in the appointment advertised. In practice the best bet — and the least time consuming — is the submission of your summary c.v. and a brief covering letter in which you draw the recipient's attention to the highly relevant experience you have had. Obviously bring out your best points but do be honest and don't claim to have done things you haven't done or put your age back five years! — you'll be caught out eventually by the pension scheme and probably lose your job without compensation.

If you don't quite match the exact specification but have very relevant experience draw this out; 'although I do not have a degree in electrical engineering I have been an associate member of the I.E.E. since 1956 (via H.N.C. and part III) and I have done exactly the same work as the graduate engineers in this design office ever since.' The employer requires knowledge and understanding of principles and the ability to apply them more than paper qualifications and often demands a degree to ensure a certain minimum standard. Of course he may have some other motive (such as acceptability to the rest of the team) but this is unlikely. When the advertiser calls for a letter of application and a c.v. he usually wants to learn not only your basic qualifications and experience but your ability to present your case clearly, concisely, and persuasively — itself an important attribute in an executive. Don't over-sell yourself; personnel men are cautious, fairly stolid people not given to sudden wild enthusiasms and most will be irritated by the hard sell.

It is vitally important, therefore, that you spend a lot of time and trouble to get your initial letter just right. Keep a copy of all your letters if you can and as time goes by look back over them and try to evaluate why some worked and some did not. One of the major reasons why people are rejected before interview is because they have submitted a scrappy, ill-prepared initial letter of application which has probably done scant justice to their very real abilities. This may seem unfair but it is a fact — especially if there is a large response, and 150 replies are common. First impressions are more important now than at any other stage; the selection process has started. Here are some tips.

1. Start by stating which job you are applying for, where the advertisement appeared and when. This will ensure that in a large organisation your letter is correctly routed.

2. If your handwriting is very difficult to read have your letter typed. Above all print your name underneath your signature.

3. Include your telephone number — the exchange and number — in case the company wishes to call you for interview quickly.

4. Use good quality paper and envelopes.

5. Lay your letter out attractively using a suitably shaped sheet of paper.

6. If you are sending a c.v. make sure that it has been neatly typed and laid out. If you cannot do this yourself there are agencies which will do it for a modest sum. Good photocopies are acceptable.

7. Do not fill your letter with heavy crossings-out or obvious corrections. It may be a bore but it will be worth your while doing it again.

8. Keep copies of your letters.

9. Apply only for the job advertised. Do not say that you are prepared to consider other vacancies if your qualifications are not quite up to the mark. If you do you have eliminated yourself already. Should there be another vacancy that might be suitable and of interest to you the interviewer will soon be in touch with you.

10. Do not go into the reasons why you left each job. No doubt you will be asked this at the interview. Be careful how you indicate your present employment situation. The simple fact 'I have been declared redundant' — or 'owing to the closure of company x I am now obliged to look for a post etc.' is quite sufficient. Don't go into rambling explanations and preferably don't mention the redundancy unless you have clearly been out of work for some time (from your c.v.). In your letter of application it looks like a defensive ploy. In letters of application it is wise to remember what Disraeli said about political

84

leadership — 'Never apologise. Never explain.'

Those forms

When you receive an application blank to complete — in spite of your very comprehensive c.v. — don't just scribble in the principal details and think that's it. Application blanks seem invariably to be designed by people who have never had to complete them (or they live in nameless houses in cities with two-line addresses or have very little imagination). Space when it is most needed is at a premium (and vice versa); questions are repetitious or obscure; and there is either insufficient room to do justice to yourself — or else you are faced with four blank pages to fill! Very off-putting! It is vital, therefore, to study the form in detail before starting to fill it in. If you can, take a photocopy and use that both as a draft and your file copy. Always draft out your replies to the narrative questions to ensure that what you say is relevant and gives as much fact as possible. If space allows it is worth typing your replies for ease of duplication but this requires considerable patience and care. (Many forms are not consistent in their lay-out . . . and lining up the boxes is often a work of art.) Above all write clearly — most forms are photocopied these days so that each interviewer has one. Do answer *every* question; the form will be returned to you if not and valuable time will have been lost. In practice you need to allow 2-3 hours to complete an application blank, though there are some which can be done in under half an hour. It is permissible to put additional details (or to continue the answer to a question) on a separate sheet of paper if space really is at a premium — but keep it brief; you run the risk of it being detached.

When returning your completed application blank send a brief covering letter as a matter of courtesy. It is quite a good idea to indicate when you could or could not attend for interview in the next three weeks, but don't make it too complicated or unnecessarily hard to fit in. The addition of the phrase 'I look forward to meeting you (or Mr. —) in the near future' leaves a courteous impression.

If you don't get a single interview after all this you are clearly applying for the wrong jobs!

7   Consultancies, Agencies and others who can help you

Apart from friends and personal contacts you can also get help from a wide range of other sources. It is not generally realised, for instance, that many employment agencies also conduct a continuous search for executives on behalf of their corporate clients or that they may maintain a register of available personnel which they mail regularly to companies who are on the look-out for good men thinking of making a move. In any case, most executive recruitment agencies will give a little free advice to individuals who fall within their sphere of activity; they will be able to tell you about such factors as the state of the job market and the going salary for the type of appointment you are looking for. In other words their operation is not confined to the kind of definite assignment — looking for a man to fill a particular job — which one associates with the appearance of their names in the job advertisement sections of the press.

If you feel unsure about the direction which your career ought to be taking you may consider seeking impartial advice on a more professional basis than that which your friends are qualified to give. In that case you might think about going and talking to a vocational guidance service. For a relatively modest fee — somewhere between £20 and £30 — they will interview you and give you tests, questionnaires and counselling to establish where you can best apply your abilities. Possibly they may advise you — or you yourself may decide — that you need further formal qualifications, or even re-training for a new career. Whether this is a practicable step depends on your age and commitments, but there is in fact a wide range of full-time and part-time courses available to mature students in polytechnics and colleges.

The information on these various sources of advice is widely scattered and in this chapter we have provided a thumbnail reference to the main firms and organisations that

What you always suspected about job-finding...

In every walk of life, some people seem to find plum jobs almost automatically, while others appear to spend their lives chasing opportunities which always manage to elude them. As you may well suspect, the reason rarely relates to mere luck.

Very easily, very soon, you could be receiving a continual stream of opportunities, pre-matched to your qualifications, aptitudes and experience. Simply by taking advantage, totally free of cost, of Lansdowne's Appointments Register – which covers practically every conceivable career path.

Complete the coupon now and you will receive your registration form by return. From there on in, those interviews will be chasing you ! . . .

To: Stuart Tait, Lansdowne Appointments Register, Design House, The Mall, London W5 5LS. Tel: 01-579 6585 (anytime – 24 hour answering service)

lansdowne
Appointments Register

are likely to be of interest to anybody thinking of changing their job. It is divided into two sections. The first is a simple alphabetical list, showing names and addresses which are keyed as follows:

Management Training Courses	MTC
Executive Search	ES
Selection Consultants	SC
Vocational Guidance	VG
Registers	ER
Employment Agencies	EA
Franchise Consultants	FC
Professional Body	PB

The second section consists of reference advertisements, classified by region, from companies, organisations and educational bodies who have given further information which readers are likely to find helpful.

Alphabetical list of consultancies and other organisations

Accord Staff Agency Ltd   EA
34/36 Maddox Street
London W1R 9PD

Accountancy Personnel Ltd   EA
65 Moorgate
London EC2

Regional Offices:
14 Temple Street
Birmingham

49 King Street
Manchester

Agro Management Consultants Ltd   SC MTC
692 Warwick Road
Solihull
Warwickshire

Subsidiary of P-E Consulting Group Ltd
Also offices in London, Egham, Altrincham, Newcastle,
Glasgow, Belfast and overseas

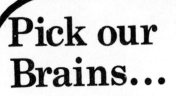
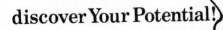

Alangate Employment Agency Ltd* VG EA
Alangate House
6 Great Queen Street
Holborn
London WC2B 5DG

Associated companies:

Accountancy Engagements
78 Queen Victoria Street
London EC1N 4SI

Alangate Industrial Agency
12 City Road
London EC1Y 2AA

Alangate (Stockbroking, Financial & Banking Div) Perm Dept
9-11 Poultry
London EC2R 8EI

Paterson Employment Agency
20 Queen Victoria Street
London EC4N 4SY

*See also page 89

Anglian Regional Management Centre* MTC
North East London Polytechnic
Danbury Park
Danbury
Chelmsford
Essex CM3 4AT

*See also page 173

Appointment Aids (Luton) Ltd ES SC ER EA
2 Manchester Street
Luton
Bedfordshire LU1 2QB

Associated company:

Find-A-Job (Luton) Ltd

The Arens Group   ES
375 City Road
London EC1V 1NA

Argus Appointments (Computer Personnel) Ltd   EA
31 Kingly Street
London W1R 6JJ

Regional offices:

1-3 St Paul's Churchyard
London EC4M 8AU

Ashley Associates*   ES SC ER
75 Mosley Street
Manchester M2 3HR

Regional offices:

35/38 Portman Square
London W1H 7FH

20 Coates Crescent
Edinburgh EH3 7AF

*See also page 120

Association of Supervisory & Executive Engineers ER
Appointments Bureau
Wix Hill House
West Horsley
Leatherhead
Surrey

B.S.B. Appointments Ltd   SC EA
(Senior Appointments Div. of Brook Street Bureau Group)
47 Davies Street
London W1

Offices also at:

63 Oxford Street
London W1R 1RB (Sales/Marketing)

34/35 High Holborn
London WC1Y 6AA (Legal & Accounting)

44 Bow Lane
London EC34 H9DT (Insurance & Stockbroking)

11 Kingsgate Parade
London SW1E 5NE (Computers & Engineering)

32 The Strand
London WC2N 6MA (Professional)

67 High Street, Wood Green
London N22 6BH (Professional)

150 Fleet Street
London EC4 2DQ (Professional)

British Association for Commercial & Industrial Education
16 Park Crescent   MTC
London W1N 4AP

Bernadette Bureau
55 New Bond Street   EA
London W1Y 0ND

Boyden International Ltd*
11/15 Arlington Street   ES
London SW1

See also page 111

Bristol Polytechnic
(see South West Regional Management Centre)

British Transport Staff College
Hook Heath Road   MTC
Woking
Surrey

Building Associates Ltd
11 Muswell Hill
London N10

Associated company:

Personnel Associates
76 London Road
Chelmsford
Essex

Bull, Holmes Ltd　　　　　　　　　　　　　SC
25/27 Oxford Street
London W1R 1RF

C.S.L. Group Ltd　　　　　　　　　　　SC ER
4 Lampton Road
Hounslow
Middlesex

Associated companies:

Advance Selection Ltd
Commercial Selection Ltd
C.S.L. Management Consultants Ltd
Senior Executive Development Association

**Cambell-Johnstone (Management Recruitment
Consultants) Ltd**　　　　　　　　　　　　　SC
35 New Broad Street
London EC2M 1NH

Associated companies:

Cambell-Johnstone Advertising Ltd
Cambell-Johnstone Executive Secretaries Ltd

Canny Bowen & Associates Ltd　　　　　　ES
83 Pall Mall
London SW1Y 5ES

Associated companies:

Canny Bowen Howard Peck & Associates Inc
425 Park Avenue
New York
New York 10022 U.S.A.

Canny Bowen & Associates S.A.
214 Avenue Louise
1050 Brussels, Belgium

Career Analysts*   SC VG MTC
Career House
90 Gloucester Place
London W1H 4BL

*See also page 111

Career Plan Ltd   SC VG ER
7 Wine Office Court
London EC4A 3BY

Offices also at:

106 Fenchurch Street
London EC3M 5JB (Insurance)

17 Air Street
London W1R 5RJ (Female Executive & Secretarial)

Arthur Carr & Partners Employment Agency   EA
1 Robert Street
The Adelphi
London WC2

Caterers & Hotel Advisers Ltd   ES SC
5 Stratford Place
London W1N 0DX

Central Staff Agency   EA
9 Duke Street
Cardiff

City Desk Services Co Ltd   SC EA
94 Market Street
Manchester 1

Regional office:

5 Claremont Road, Sale, Cheshire

College of Preceptors   PB
Bloomsbury House
130 High Holborn
London WC1V 6PS

Consulting Partners S.A.   ES
34 Dover Street
London W1X 4QX

Offices also in Europe and the Americas

Context Training   SC MTC
29 Old Bond Street
London W1

Associated company:

The Oxford Consultants
Greyfriars House
Henton
Oxford

Criterion Appointments Ltd*   ER
Queens House
Leicester Square
London WC2

*See also page 112

Directors' Secretaries Ltd   EA
27 Old Bond Street
London W1X 3AA

Drayton Secretarial   EA
4 Horton Road
West Drayton
Middlesex UB7 8ED

Associated company:

Jays Jobbery (Staines) Ltd
156 High Street
Staines, Middlesex

The Eldon Bureau   EA
1 Eldon Square
Newcastle upon Tyne NE1 7JG

Essex Appointments Ltd   EA
Wenley House
23/25 New London Road
Chelmsford
Essex CM2 0NA

Regional office:

112a Southchurch Road
Southend
Essex SS1 2LX (specialising shipping staff)

Europa Agency Ltd   SC EA
10 Corn Exchange
Leeds 1

Associated company:

Modern Era Employment Agency
Holly Park Mills
Calverley
Pudsey
Yorkshire

European College of Marketing & Marketing Research   MTC
9 Aston Road
Nuneaton
Warwickshire

Euroselection Ltd*   ES SC
109 Marine Parade
Brighton
Sussex

*See also page 178

Executemps   EA
21/22 Poland Street
London W1V 3DD

Executive Advertising Ltd   SC
8a Symons Street
Sloane Square
London SW3 2TJ

Associated companies:

Executive Search Ltd
Executive Search International Ltd
Executive Search International S.A., Paris
Executive Search International, Spain

The Executive Aide Register   ER
114 Station Road East
Oxted
Surrey

Executive Career Ltd*   ES SC
Palmcroy House
387 London Road
Croydon CR0 3PB
Surrey

Associated company:
Executive Care
See also page 89

Exsel Executive Selection Ltd   SC
Warwick Chambers
707a Warwick Road
Solihull
Warwickshire

John Figes & Partners Ltd*   ES SC ER
200 Old Brompton Road
London SW5 0BT
See also pages 65 and 112

The Fosse Bureau   EA
9a Princes Street
Yeovil
Somerset

Office also at:

27a Silver Street
Taunton
Somerset

Franchise Advisory Centre Ltd*   FC
160 Piccadilly
London W1
*See also pages 112 and 173

The Glacier Institute of Management   MTC
17 King Edward's Road
Ruislip
Middlesex HA4 7AF

Glamorgan Polytechnic   MTC
Llantwit Road
Treforest
Pontypridd
Glamorgan

Graduate Appointments Register*   ER
76 Dean Street
London W1

Associated companies:

Accountancy Appointments Register
Computer Appointments Register
Electronics Appointments Register
Engineering Appointments Register
Professional Appointments Register
Sales & Marketing Appointments Register
Scientific Appointments Register

*See also page 113

Graduate Girls*   ES SC ER EA
116 Brompton Road
London SW3
*See also page 113

H.B. Executive ER
21/22 Poland Street
London W1V 3DD

Regional offices in Birmingham, Bristol, Leeds,
Newcastle, Manchester and Glasgow

H.M.R. Employment Bureau Ltd ER EA
175a High Street
Poole
Dorset BH15 1AZ

Heidrick & Struggles Inc ES
41 Dover Street
London W1

Offices also in Belgium and U.S.A.

Hoggett Bowers & Partners Ltd ES SC VG
21/22 Poland Street
London W1V 3DD

Regional offices in Birmingham, Bristol, Leeds,
Newcastle, Manchester and Glasgow

The Holly Agency EA
Observer Buildings
Rowbottom Square
Wigan
Lancashire

Associated company:

James A. Longley & Staff Ltd
(Business and Management Consultants)
see above address, and also at:—

The Court, Pencoed
Glamorgan

Independent Assessment & Research SC VG MTC
Centre Ltd
57 Marylebone High Street
London W1M 3AE

Inplan Ltd   ES SC MTC
Fillongley
Coventry
Warwickshire

Associated companies:

G.F.M. Chemical Market Research Ltd
C.M.R. Chemical Market Research Ltd
Industron Ltd

International Executives S.A.R.L.   ER
Re-locating offices from Grayshott, Surrey
to Central London

Kiernan & Company Inc (U.K.) Ltd   ES SC
73/75 Mortimer Street
London W1N 7TB

Associated companies:

Kiernan & Company B.V., Amsterdam
Kiernan & Co. Inc, New York & Washington

Kingston Polytechnic   MTC
Penrhyn Road
Kingston upon Thames KT1 2EE

Korn/Ferry Dickinson Ltd*   ES
20 Queen Street
Mayfair
London W1X 7PJ

Offices also in Brussels, Paris, Tokyo and U.S.A.

*See also page 8

Lansdowne Recruitment Ltd*   SC ER EA
Design House
The Mall
London W5 5LS

Associated companies:
Career Girl Ltd

100

Lansdowne Publications Ltd

*See also pages 87 and 113

Robert Lee International Manpower
Consultants Ltd   ES SC VG ER
24 Berkeley Square
London W1

Offices also in Brussels, Dublin, Paris, Munich,
Johannesburg, New York and San Francisco

Letchworth College of Technology   MTC
Broadway
Letchworth
Hertfordshire SG6 3PB

Loughborough University of Technology   MTC
Centre for Extension Studies
University of Technology
Loughborough
Leicestershire LE11 3TU

M.D. Selection Services   SC
Method Development Group
10 Woodhouse Square
Leeds LS3 1AF

M.S.L. Group Ltd   SC
17 Stratton Street
London W1X 6DB

Offices also in Birmingham, Manchester,
Edinburgh, Glasgow, Belfast

Associated companies:

HAY-MSL Ltd
Judy Farquharson Ltd

Malestaff Ltd   EA
16 Berkeley Street
London W1X 5AE

Office also at:

362 Euston Road
London NW1 3BL

Malla Technical Staff Ltd   ER EA
334 Euston Road
London NW1 3BG

Management Consultants Association   SC MTC
23/24 Cromwell Place
London SW7 2LG

Management on the Move Ltd*   ER
21 Godliman Street
London EC4V 5BD
See also page 113

Management Personnel*   ER
2 Tunsgate
Guildford Surrey
See also page 114

Management Training Consultants   MTC
214 Saint Nicholas Circle
Leicester LE1 4LD

Marketing Improvements Ltd   SC
7 Kendall Place
Blandford Street
London W1H 3AG

Office also in Brussels

Charles Martin Associates Ltd*   ES SC
23 College Hill
London EC4

Regional office:

Bridge House, Hunningham, Leamington Spa, Warwickshire
See also page 114

Maylands Staff Bureau   ER EA
1 Bank Court
Hemel Hempstead
Hertfordshire

William Messenger & Associates   SC TO
26 Cambridge Avenue
New Malden
Surrey KT3 4LE

Modern Business Services (Wales) Ltd   SC ER
P O Box 20
High Street
Newport
Monmouthshire

Regional offices:

2 Quay Street
Bristol

67/77 Queen Street
Cardiff CF1 4BD

Montague Kent & Co Ltd   SC VG ER MTC
11 Argyll Street
London W1V 1AB

Associated company:

Francis M.S. Muller & Associates Ltd
Industrial Psychologists

Motor Trade Selection   SC
7a Grafton Street
London W1

Associated company:

Ronald Sewell & Associates Ltd
Bath

Mount Staff Bureau   EA
4 The Mount
Guildford
Surrey

Office also at:

Brook House
Alencon Link
Basingstoke
Hampshire

National Advisory Centre on Careers for Women   VG
251 Brompton Road
London SW3 2HB

North East London Polytechnic
(see Anglian Regional Management Centre)

Northern Employment Services Ltd   SC ER EA
19 Richmond Terrace
Blackburn
Lancashire BB1 7BL

Offices also at:

9 Railway Road
Blackburn BB1 5AX

12 Boot Way
Burnley BB11 2EE

28 Market Street
Bury

Stamford House
98 Bradshawgate
Bolton

Odgers & Co Ltd*   ES SC ER
Adelaide House
London Bridge
London EC4R 9DS
See also page 115

ORES International Ltd ES
35/39 Maddox Street
London W1R 9LD

Parent company:

ORES S.A., Paris

Richard Owen Associates* EA
47 Finsbury Pavement
London EC2A 1HT

Associated company:

Richard Owen & Harper
9-11 Finsbury Court
Finsbury Pavement
London EC2A 1HT

See also page 115

P-E Consulting Group SC ER EA TO
14/20 Headfort Place
London SW1

Offices also in Solihull, Altrincham,
Newcastle-upon-Tyne, Glasgow, Belfast and Dublin

Personnel Associates SC
(Petroleum and Petrochemical Personnel Consultants)
76 London Road
Chelmsford
Essex

Personnel Placement Services Ltd ES SC ER
37 Great James Street, London WC1

Plumbley/Endicott & Associates ES SC
Premier House
150 Southampton Row
London WC1B 5AL

Polyglot Agency for Linguists   EA
Bank Chambers
214 Bishopsgate
London EC2M 4Q

Portsmouth Management Centre*   MTC
Portsmouth Polytechnic
141 High Street
Portsmouth PO1 2HY

*See also page 118

Price Waterhouse Associates   SC
31/41 Worship Street
London EC2A 2HD

Offices also in Bristol, Birmingham,
Newcastle-upon-Tyne and Manchester

Regular Forces Employment Association   EA
25 Bloomsbury Square
London WC1A 2LN

Also 42 other offices throughout United Kingdom

Russel, Ewbank & Partners Ltd   SC
Prudential House
North Street
Brighton
Sussex BN1 1RW

St Paul's Employment Agency Ltd   EA
Avon House
360/366 Oxford Street
London W1N 9HA

Sales Associates   SC
Queens House
28 Kingsway
London WC2B 6JR

Regional office:
416 Royal Exchange
Manchester M2

Sales Selection Ltd   ES SC TO
35/37 Grosvenor Gardens House
Grosvenor Gardens
London SW1

Associated companies:

Eastern Advisory Services Ltd
D.V.A. Training Ltd
Tilburn Day Associates Ltd
Tilburn Day Blake Ltd

Senior Secretaries Ltd   EA
173 New Bond Street
London W1Y 9PB

Solihull Staff Agency   EA
Warwick Chambers
707a Warwick Road
Solihull
Warwickshire

Associated companies:

Redditch Staff Agency
Beech House
Church Green East
Redditch
Worcestershire

Sheldon Staff Agency
2070 Coventry Road
Birmingham B26 3HR

Spa Staff Agency
27a Waterloo Place
Leamington Spa
Warwickshire

Rotherham Staff Bureau Ltd
17 Moorgate Street
Rotherham
Yorkshire

The South West Regional Management Centre*   MTC
Bristol Polytechnic
Felixstowe House
Clifton
Bristol BS8 3NP

See also page 117

Stroud, Morgan*   ES SC VG ER MTC
160, Piccadilly
London W1V 9DF

See also pages 65 and 115

T.W. Management Consultants Ltd   ES SC MTC
27 Princes Road
Clevedon
Somerset BS21 7SY

Associated company:

T.W. School of Management Ltd
(address as above)

Talent Brokers Ltd*   SC
20 Maddox Street
London W1R 9PG

Associated company:

Talbro Advertising Ltd

See also page 116

Christopher Tilly & Associates   ES
19 Bentinck Street
London W1

Associated companies in Paris, Frankfurt, Brussels, Milan.

University of Lancaster
School of Management & Organisational Sciences
Lancaster LA1 4YR

MTC

Vocational Guidance Centre
2 Mosley Street
Manchester 2

VG

Watford College of Technology
Department of Management Studies
Hempstead Road
Watford
Hertfordshire WD1 3EZ

MTC

J. Watson Sanderson Ltd
70 Queen Victoria Street
London EC4N 4SJ

ES SC

Western Executives
4/6 The Colonnade
High Street
Maidenhead
Berkshire SL6 1QL

SC ER

Western Girl Ltd
262 Regent Street
London W1

EA

Regional offices throughout England

Western Men International*
27 Kymberley Road
Harrow
Middlesex

EA

See also page 116

West One Selection Group of Companies
Including Sales Personnel (U.K.) Ltd and
West One Engineering
11 Dryden Chambers

SC EA

119 Oxford Street
London W1R 1PA

Regional office:

West One Selection (Bristol) Ltd
52 Park Street
Bristol BS1 5JN

Western Personnel Ltd*　　　　　　　ES SC ER MTC
3 Whiteladies Road
Bristol BS8 1NU

*See also page 119

Whitehead Recruitment Ltd　　　　　　SC ER
Whitehead Consulting Group
21 Wigmore Street
London W1H 9LA

Offices also in Amsterdam, Brussels, Dusseldorf,
Oslo, Milan and Paris

Young People's & Executive Employment Agency　　EA
10 North Street
Guildford
Surrey

Egon Zehnder International　　　　　　ES SC
87 Jermyn Street
London SW1Y 6JD

Offices also in Europe, Australia & Japan

Associate companies:

Zehnder & Clark International, Chicago & Los Angeles
William H. Clark Associates Inc, New York

Regional list of consultancies and other organisations

(London offices are sometimes given under regional headings because companies offer a nationwide service.)

LONDON AND SOUTH EAST

Ashley Associates
Appleby House
46 St James's Place
London SW1
Tel 01-226 3491

(See main entry page 120)

Boyden International Ltd
11/15 Arlington Street
London SW1
Tel 01-629 5986

Boyden International Ltd. Management Consultants specializing in executive search. We are the oldest and largest firm of our kind operating on a worldwide basis. We locate and place executives within many leading British companies, who regard our services as the means of making a sound investment in carefully selected individuals.

Career Analysts
Career House
90 Gloucester Place
London W1H 4BL
Tel 01-935 5452/3

Career Analysts is the leading Career Guidance organisation in the country. Our service includes tests of aptitude, interest and personality, consultation with one of our psychologists and full report. Our assessment offers applicants a chance to take stock on all aspects of career planning, obtaining qualifications, submitting applications and discovering fresh opportunities. Fee £25 — Contact us for free brochure.

Criterion Appointments Ltd
Queens House
Leicester Square
London WC2
Tel 01-734 3388

Criterion Appointments Ltd specialises in Banking, Engineering, Insurance, Property and Accountancy posts. Client companies are legion and range all over the U.K. and overseas. Large numbers of vacancies are listed and new ones are registered daily. The service is free to applicants and completely confidential. Ring us to discuss it.

John Figes & Partners Ltd
200 Old Brompton Road,
Kensington
London SW5 0BT
Tel 01-370 4345

John Figes is an independent management consultant concerned only with personnel management and especially with executive selection. He is always interested to hear from qualified and experienced executives and will advise them, without charge, on career development possibilities. The practice is retained as personnel advisers by a number of perfumery and flavour houses and is especially interested in men and women who have creative or management experience or who are technically qualified in aroma chemistry.

Franchise Advisory Centre
160 Piccadilly
London W1
Tel 01-499 0007

The Centre was established in 1967 to provide advice and information for the man who wants a business of his own. A franchise provides the benefit of help in planning and siting, and the availability of continuing assistance in management under an established brand name. However, a franchised business opportunity which offers these advantages needs

112

experienced analysis and careful investigation to ensure that the investor is suited by experience and aptitude, that his capital is protected and that his future income is assured. The first step is to arrange an initial consultation (free to Readers) with the Director.

See also page 173

Graduate Appointments Registers
75 Dean Street
London W1
Tel 01-636 3600

The seven Graduate Appointment Registers established 10 years ago are used by virtually every major company in the U.K., often to fill vacancies which are never advertised. The Registers exist for professional, executive and technical staff throughout the U.K. at salary range £2,000-£10,000. Over 100 vacancies per week are processed, the service is completely confidential and absolutely free of charge.

Lansdowne Appointments Register
Design House
The Mall
London W5 5LS
Tel 01-579 6585

The Lansdowne Appointments Register has established itself as one of the most effective ways of assessing your market value. Advice and career guidance is still free and the career summary questionnaire can be completed at home. Lansdowne's candidate selection system is increasingly relied upon by progressive employers in every field.

Management On The Move Ltd
21 Godliman Street
London EC4V 5BD
Tel 01-236 0412/7712

Nature of Service:
Advice — placement in industry and commerce — worldwide basis

Methods Used:
Interview — provision of facilities for communicating with employers, by means of a publication regularly issued. Distribution 1,000+ company subscription £100 per annum.
Eligibility:
All executives
Cost:
Initial advising interview free, communication service £25 + VAT to be charged to the individual or the company. No appointment fees to employers.
Further developments:
Five regional companies will be set up during 1974, so that our operation will become nation-wide.

Management Personnel
2 Tunsgate
Guildford
Surrey
Tel Guildford 65566

Consultants: Commercial — S. Rowley
Technical — A. Hollowell

Provides comprehensive service for the appointment of executive, middle and first line management in the commercial and engineering fields. Operates within 30 mile radius of Guildford and nationally through our subsidiaries. No fees to candidates.

Charles Martin Associates Ltd
23 College Hill
London EC4
Tel 01-248 1709

Specialists in the selection of senior executives to match appointments in industry, commerce and the professions — both in the U.K. and abroad. These may be permanent posts that cannot be filled by internal promotion or short-term appointments to deal with specific tasks. Increasingly concerned as management consultants to advise the smaller company, particularly in the field of top management organisation and appraisal.

Odgers & Co Ltd
Adelaide House
London Bridge
London EC4R 9DS
Tel 01-626 1086

Odgers and Company specialises in senior executive recruitment in the Financial and Marketing fields and those General Management areas where a strong background in either of these two disciplines is required. It provides the means of bringing together rapidly and discreetly:—
1. Able young executives who feel that the development of their careers over the next few years might well include the possibility of a move to a bigger job in another company and
2. Companies wishing to fill senior positions, usually in the £5,000 to £15,000 salary range.

Richard Owen Associates
47 Finsbury Court
Finsbury Pavement
London EC2A 1HT
Tel 01-628 8860

Richard Owen Associates specialises in accountancy vacancies in Commerce & Industry and Public Practice.
The range covered is wide, and as well as positions for experienced, qualified men, it includes opportunities for newly and part qualified accountants, trainees and book-keepers.
The company offers **FREE LISTS** of current vacancies on request and you are welcome to ring, write or call for one of these — the office is only 150 yards from Moorgate Tube Station.

Stroud Morgan
160 Piccadilly
London W1V 9DF
Tel 01-499 0007

We handle executive search, selection, vocational guidance,

executive register, self marketing and training in the U.K. and overseas. Write or ring to tell us how we can help you promptly.

(See also page 65)

Talent Brokers Ltd
20 Maddox Street
London W1R 9PG
Tel 01-499 4288

Talent Brokers offer a full assessment and selection service for the recruitment of executives in the £2,000 to £8,000 per annum range. Their clients are, in the main, fast moving consumer goods manufacturers and advertising agencies.

Western Men International
27 Kymberley Road,
Harrow
Middlesex
Tel 01-863 6668

Nature of Service: Specialises in NW & W London and Middlesex areas. Job seekers are interviewed, advised and introduced to possible employers.
To Whom Given: Executives; Accountants; All Office staff; Engineers; Designers; Draughtsmen: & maintains register of current vacancies in area.
Fees: No fees for this service.

MIDLANDS

Graduate Appointments Registers
76 Dean Street
London W1
Tel 01-636 3600

(see main entry page 113)

Lansdowne Appointments Register
Design House
The Mall
London W5 5LS
Tel 01-579 6585

(see main entry page 113)

Charles Martin Associates Ltd
23 College Hill
London EC4
Tel 01-248 1709

(see main entry page 114)

Odgers & Co Ltd
Adelaide House
London Bridge
London EC4R 9DS
Tel 01-626 1086

(see main entry page 115)

Western Personnel Ltd
3 Whiteladies Road
Bristol BS8 1NU
Tel 0272 30255

(see main entry page 119)

SOUTH WEST

The South West Regional Management Centre
Bristol Polytechnic
Felixstowe House
Clifton Down
Bristol BS8 3NP ·
Tel 0272 311468

Bristol Polytechnic's Regional Management Centre provides
courses leading to nationally recognised management

qualifications. The range of courses is designed to meet the needs of all levels of practising and potential managers. Courses are run for full-time and part-time students, together with a variety of purpose-designed short courses. Courses available include those in business and management studies, personnel administration, marketing, production management (work study, purchasing and supply, materials handling, etc) and public services management (education, the health service, local government, etc). For further information please write, stating your particular interest, to: The South West Regional Management Centre, Bristol Polytechnic, Felixstowe House, Clifton Down Bristol BS8 3NP or telephone Bristol (0272) 311468.

Graduate Appointments Registers
76 Dean Street
London W1
Tel 01-636 3600

(see main entry page 113)

Lansdowne Appointments Register
Design House
The Mall
London W5 5LS
Tel 01-579 6585

(see main entry page 113)

Odgers & Co Ltd
Adelaide House
London Bridge
London EC4R 9DS
Tel 01-626 1086

(see main entry page 115)

Portsmouth Management Centre
141 High Street
Old Portsmouth
Portsmouth PO1 2HY
Tel 0705 812611

The Portsmouth Management Centre as well as running customer designed courses, offers the following which are of particular interest to those changing their jobs:

The Portsmouth Executive Development Programme
A task orientated programme for middle and higher management. Six weeks residential in three two-week stages with in-company projects.

Introduction to Management
A two-week residential course for professional staff and newly-appointed managers.

Training Officer Course
A series of eight one-week modules which may be taken as a whole with an in-company project to launch a new trainee in his first post, or selected individually according to need by the more experienced training officer.

Western Personnel Ltd
3 Whiteladies Road
Bristol BS8 1NU
Tel 0272 30255

Now established as leading recruitment consultancy for the West, South West and South Wales, whose staff combine some 50 years personnel experience in the area: in recent years have probably handled more professional, managerial and technical appointments (salaries £2,000-£8,000) than any other commercial practice in the region.

NORTH EAST

Graduate Appointments Registers
76 Dean Street
London W1
Tel 01-636 3600

(see main entry page 113)

Lansdowne Appointments Register
Design House
The Mall
London W5 5LS
Tel 01-579 6585

(see main entry page 113)

Odgers & Co Ltd
Adelaide House
London Bridge
London EC4R 9DS
Tel 01-626 1086

(see main entry page 115)

NORTH WEST

Ashley Associates
75 Mosley Street
Manchester M2 3HR
Tel 061-236 0987

Ashley Associates is a division of Knight Wegenstein Ltd., an international group of consultants. With offices in Manchester, London and Edinburgh, complete U.K. coverage can be given. We undertake executive recruitment consultancy for appointments at all levels including top executives.

Graduate Appointments Registers
76 Dean Street
London W1
Tel 01-636 3600

(see main entry page 113)

Lansdowne Appointments Register
Design House
The Mall, London W5 5LS
Tel 01-579 6585

(see main entry page 113)

120

Odgers & Co Ltd
Adelaide House
London Bridge
London EC4R 9DS
Tel 01-626 1086

(see main entry page 115)

SCOTLAND

Ashley Associates
20 Coates Crescent
Edinburgh EH3 7AF
Tel 031-226 3491

(see main entry page 120)

Graduate Appointments Registers
76 Dean Street
London W1
Tel 01-636 3600

(see main entry page 113)

Lansdowne Appointments Register
Design House
The Mall
London W5 5LS
Tel 01-579 6585

(see main entry page 113)

Odgers & Co Ltd
Adelaide House
London Bridge
London EC4R 9DS
Tel 01-626 1086

(see main entry page 115)

121

WALES

Graduate Appointments Registers
76 Dean Street
London W1
Tel 01-636 3600

(see main entry page 113)

Lansdowne Appointments Register
Design House
The Mall
London W5 5LS
Tel 01-579 6585

(see main entry page 113)

Odgers & Co Ltd
Adelaide House
London Bridge
London EC4R 9DS
Tel 01-626 1086

(see main entry page 115)

Western Personnel Ltd
3 Whiteladies Road
Bristol BS8 1NU
Tel 0272 30255

(see main entry page 119)

NORTHERN IRELAND

Graduate Appointments Registers
76 Dean Street
London W1
Tel 01-636 3600

(see main entry page 113)

Lansdowne Appointments Register
Design House
The Mall
London W5 5LS
Tel 01-579 6585

(see main entry page 113)

Language tuition

An increasing number of appointments call for the ability to converse and negotiate in a second language. Whilst most people have learnt another language at school, this has not given them a command of the language and vocabulary of the professions, business or politics.

A thoroughly experienced international interpreter can give just this kind of intensive tuition. We know of one — but there will be others — who can give advanced tuition in French and Spanish and an introduction to German, Russian and Polish. For further details contact Mr. Philip Plumbley at Plumbley/Endicott & Associates, Premier House, 150 Southampton Row, London WC1B 5AL.

8   Résumés, application blanks and c.v.'s

There are many ways of presenting yourself to a prospective employer, from a telephone enquiry to a fully comprehensive dossier. Let us examine the principal ones you are likely to come across.

The telephone call

There are three types of situation when the initial contact will be by telephone: you may be invited to telephone direct after one of your personal contacts has paved the way; or the advertisement may invite applications by telephone — 'candidates should ring Mr. Jones on 123 456 during normal office hours or 789 923 at other times'; or you may be approached by a 'head hunter' to whom you have sent your c.v. or who may have heard in a round-about way that you are 'on the market'. The telephone is used primarily for speed, convenience or discretion. Where an appointment may be difficult to fill or candidates cannot write easily (e.g. construction engineers out on site) the telephone is considered to be the main means of recruitment.

When *you* ring it is as well to be prepared for the type of questions you are likely to be asked. Your c.v. will act as an *aide memoire* for names, dates etc. In addition try to work out what the interviewer is likely to want to know — the critical factors on which he will decide whether or not to invite you to interview. If necessary, draft out a few concise replies. Here are some typical questions and answers.

Q. *Could you give me a brief picture of yourself?*
A. Yes. I am aged 35 and have a second class Mechanical Sciences Tripos from Cambridge and have spent the last 14 years with two major engineering concerns where I have specialised in the design of steam turbines for power stations and ships. Most of my experience has been in design and

development though I did spend a period of two years seeing a new type of machine through the production workshops. For the last four years I have been Assistant Chief Engineer — Special projects with . . .

Q. *What are your professional qualifications?*

A. I have been a full member of the I.Mech.E. since 1965.

Q. *How many people do you supervise directly?*

A. 30 - mostly qualified men including 10 draughtsmen, three technical clerks and five admin staff. When a special project is approaching the production stage the production engineering staff report to me on technical matters.

Q. *I described the job to you very briefly just now. Tell me, what attracts and what are you looking for?*

A. I heard a paper read by your Mr. Robinson at an Institution seminar about six months ago and liked the sound of the work you are doing particularly in the realm of size reduction but with increased output. As you may know, this company has decided to cut back its development work and so your advertisement is of special interest to me.

Q. *How soon could you be available?*

A. Could I suggest the 1st . . .

Q. *Would there be any problems about your having to move to this area?*

A. No. Of course I should have to move house and find new schools for the children but as they are both under eight this shouldn't be a problem; and my wife isn't working.

Q. *The salary we have in mind is about £4,500: how does this compare with your present salary?*

A. It would mean a bit of a drop; I've been getting £4,750; presumably there would be scope for rises within the salary bracket?

Q. *Oh yes, the scale runs up to just over £5,500 and in any case I think that we might be able to match your present salary. Is there anything else you would like to know at this stage?*

A. No; I think you've covered the critical points and presumably everything will be gone into in detail at the interview. Would you like me to send a c.v.?

Q. *Yes please, that would be helpful. Let me see, could you be available for interview towards the end of this week —*

say Thursday?

A. Yes. The afternoon would suit me better if that's all the same to you.

Q. *Shall we say three o'clock then? I'll drop you a line to confirm it and to tell you how to get here.*

The approach 'out of the blue' from a head hunter is much more difficult to handle as it will take you unawares — even if you have sent your c.v. to a number of people. When you receive this sort of call you need to be cautious; it is easy to be carried away and to regret it later. The caller will use a semi-informal approach;

Caller. Is that George Fortescue?

GF. It is.

C. Good evening. You won't know me but my name is John Smith and we have a mutual acquaintance in Frederick Johnson of the merchant bankers. I'm a management consultant and have been asked by one of my clients to help fill a very senior appointment. From what I have heard about you I think that you might be a very strong candidate for this post. Could you be interested in making a move?

GF I see. Well yes, as a matter of fact I could. Are you able to tell me more about the job and your client at this stage?

C. Yes indeed, This is all in the very strictest confidence but my client is . . . etc.

The caller will give a brief outline of the company, the job to be done and generally try to convey the attitudes of the management as well as the scope for the new man. He will also want to know what the candidate is looking for in terms of career and financial prospects. The call will usually end with the invitation to meet and discuss the appointment in detail.

This type of phone call is difficult to handle as you don't know what is coming and so cannot be prepared. Nevertheless, the work you did earlier when you analysed your needs and your past career will be invaluable in helping you to keep your feet on the ground and enable you to answer those awkward questions, 'What exactly are you looking for?' and 'What is the minimum salary that you are prepared to accept?' It's a good idea to keep the summary chart you made of yourself within reach of the phone so that it is always to hand when required. Of course, if you are not consciously 'on the job market' you will not have gone as far as this but if you are thinking of looking around then this self-analysis, tedious though it may be, can prove to be time very well spent.

If you have contacted the executive search firms and sent them your c.v. the caller will simply concentrate on the job, the salary, whether or not you are really interested and to arrange an interview — or not. Usually, when the searcher has got to the point of giving you a ring he has virtually decided that he would like to see you.

The c.v.
The next gradation is the c.v. — curriculum vitae ('the course of your life') or 'track record' as the Americans call it. It is simply a record in chronological order of the facts of your working life and other relevant details. It should be neatly tabulated and set out on not more than two sheets of paper and it is as well to prepare or order at least 50 copies! If you cannot type it yourself (and no longer have a secretary) agencies will do this for you relatively cheaply. It should cover in order:

Heading: Curriculum Vitae
Your full name

Personal details
Date of birth   Age
Marital status   Children's ages
Home address   tel. no. (exchange and no. or London code)

Qualifications
Your highest academic attainment; whether this be G.C.E. O or A level, H.S.C. or degree, H.N.C. etc.
give subjects and degree class or distinctions
Professional qualifications.
Any other *relevant* qualifications.

Experience

List in chronological order the dates, names and addresses of companies worked for − set these out in capital letters for rapid scanning − and follow this with a *brief* synopsis of each of the posts you have held, saying what your duties were. Bring out major achievements. Avoid meaningless in-company titles; your correct title may have been 'Chief Personnel and Industrial Relations Officer − Technical and Administrative staff' − but a more meaningful title would be Staff Manager! Use quantitative data whenever possible − tonnage per month; sales t.o.; rate of cash flow; return on capital invested; number of staff; number of work or distribution outlets; profit record etc. The purpose of this section is to give the reader a feel of the type of work you have done and the environment in which it was done and the size of your job − and hence the range and depth of experience you have had.

Publications

List by title, date, name of publisher any published works whether they be books, seminar papers which have been subsequently published in a professional journal, articles in newspapers, company pamphlets etc.

Other appointments

List any other appointments of note you have held including outside business interests. Include military service, non-executive directorships, consultancies etc.

Languages

If you can conduct business in another language it is worth saying so, giving the degree of your fluency.

Outside interests

Be careful how you express your outside interests. Simply list the principal ones by activity and an indication of the depth of your interest or involvement. 'Secretary and team player for Bromsgrove Tennis Club'; or 'Play golf twice a week − 10 handicap'. If you say too much or list too many things potential employers may (rightly) conclude that you are a

9-5 man. The difficulty is that employers will interpret this section in an individual and perhaps biased way. So play safe — but don't leave it blank or he will think you're a soulless automaton who simply watches TV every evening.

Salary

As a general rule, put current or last salary and a synopsis of principal fringe benefits rather than 'salary required' unless you are prepared to move at the same salary or less. The latter, however, is tantamount to an admission that you are negotiating from a position of weakness, unless you can point to special circumstances, as may indeed be the case with an older executive who no longer has children to support or an ex-serviceman who has a substantial pension. Thus, a good reason for accepting a lateral or downward move in salary should always be given.

You will note that no reasons are given for leaving jobs principally because the decision to move is a complex one. Rarely is there one overriding reason and you will want to stress different factors to different interviewers in different situations. Also, even if there are any skeletons in the cupboard, there is no need to parade them in public! Salary progression is best left out as it can so easily be misinterpreted. So much depends on the interviewer's intimate knowledge of salary scales, the purchasing power of the pound and other factors such as local pay rates, company policy, location and so on. Besides, you may have moved deliberately for less money to a rural area in order to gain first-rate experience.

This c.v. can be used for almost any job; it is factual and gives the critical information most employers want to know. You will note that nothing has been said to bring out any special experience and no references or names of referees have been given as these are all variables.

The résumé

This will vary considerably with the type and level of job and can be the bare bones of the c.v. or a long, narrative account of your main achievements written up with a special bias.

The sales/marketing man will write a special one for each company selling himself by drawing out all his relevant experience — and supressing the rest! He will blow his own trumpet and sell himself hard — and this will be expected of him; if he can't sell himself what chance is there that he will be able to sell the company's products? The more senior man will prefer the softer sell and treat it as a letter; others will prefer to use a gimmick (advertising people are especially prone to this) or the form of a report. The older man will give more weight to the last 15 years and only an outline of earlier experience. In other words these will vary considerably, are highly selective and depend very much on the job. In essence the candidate is selecting himself for the job by showing how closely he meets the requirements and by bringing out any bonus he can offer. The assessor will also study it for gaps and inconsistencies.

A good résumé should be interesting to read. Everything it says — or omits to say — is of interest to the employer and so is the way it is presented and expressed. Fortunately, by now, you have all the raw data you need from your detailed self-analysis to tackle this hurdle. Every time you sit down to write one it will be worthwhile referring to the original analysis partly to keep your feet on the ground, partly so that nothing of importance is forgotten, and partly because it will trigger off other ideas. Probably the best way to tackle a narrative résumé is to put yourself in the interviewer's shoes and ask yourself what you would want to read. To summarise:

1. Make it interesting. Use plenty of paragraphs and keep to one topic at a time. A mere collection of facts is meaningless unless related to the background of the company; a rambling prosy recital is simply not read beyond the first page. Make it easy to take in and make it flow so that it can be scanned quickly.

2. Highlight the important points. Don't clutter it with trivia and irrelevancies or vital facts will be lost in the verbiage.

3. Give it an overall shape so that the reader can go back and pick out points of interest later without having to wade through page after page.

4.   It is a good idea to work out a plan beforehand. Reduce each paragraph to one sentence — that is the point you want to make. Then illustrate it with factual references.

5.   If you have time draft your résumé in full. In this way you will be able to make it sharper and livelier by taking out anything that is prosy or irrelevant.

6.   *Always* read it over for errors (your wife will spot spelling and grammatical errors too).

7.   If you have difficulty with your style of writing get a friend to help you with the early ones and then use these as models for the rest.

The dossier

If you decide to apply for a job abroad — especially in the U.S.A. or continental Europe — you will need to produce a Personal Dossier. The international organisations such as the I.L.O. warn British applicants that many otherwise excellent candidates are rejected without interview because they give too little information. If you are in any doubt as to the form your application should take contact the appropriate Embassy — the commercial counsellor will readily advise you.

To begin with, your dossier needs a good cover that won't show the dirt. Ideally, you should Letraset your name on the front with the words 'Personal Dossier — Confidential'. Choose either a cover with a clap pocket or one with the means of keeping the papers in order and undamaged. The inside should be divided into sections: Personal Details; Education and Training; Work Record; Other Interests; Publications; Testimonials. You will also need a good passport photograph which should be affixed inside a transparent envelope securely on the inside front cover. Make sure that your name and address is on the back of the photo in case it is separated from the file at any time. Lay out the dossier as you would a special report. Use separate sheets of paper with headings for each section and space things out attractively. Include photocopies of your actual degree or other certificates such as professional memberships, and, where possible, written testimonials of your work — you may have to ask for these. Make this a comprehensive affair. 'Personal Details' will include height,

131

weight, health record; information about your family — ages, names of children, your wife's maiden name and nationality; where you were both born; N.I. number, bank account no. — in short any information a future employer might need. The work record should start with a single sheet summary of all the jobs and positions held in chronological order with dates. Then you will need to do a detailed break-down of each job using organisation charts and giving details of accountabilities, actual duties, allocation of time and so on. Of course, you will only need to do one of these as a photocopy could always be made if an employer wishes to retain part of it. Usually you will take this with you to interview although it might have to be sent by registered post.

Application blanks

The good application blank is a useful selection tool; the bad one a twentieth-century, refined instrument of torture! If you strongly suspect that an application blank will be sent irrespective of what you may have said in your initial letter, send a brief letter of application and enclose a photocopied c.v. — just in case. Nothing is more soul-destroying than having spent hours on a résumé to receive back an application blank and standard covering letter from a secretary.

Application blanks tend to fall into three categories: the personal profile; the general purpose personnel; those devised by psychologists.

1. The personal profile

This is the simplest form of application blank. It was originally designed by one of the authors and is based on the summary a personnel man will usually make of any letter of application. Strictly, it was conceived as a combined letter of application and outline c.v. It contains just enough information for the personnel man to decide whether you are a 'possible' or an 'outright reject'. The form has the advantage of speed (from both points of view) and ensures that the critical information is received first time. It can be completed literally in 15 minutes. The usual procedure is for the advertisement to say 'candidates should ring 123 456 or write for further information and a Personal Profile'.

The information you receive has been drawn up to enable you to get a feel of the company as well as the facts of the job. The end result is that those who complete the profile are 'good' candidates. Some employers will interview on the strength of this information; others will invite you to interview but ask you to complete a much more searching document in the meantime. It is worth making sure that you give *all* the information asked for in the profile as only the bare essentials are asked but don't go into long explanations; just stick to the facts.

2. The general purpose personnel

There is an enormous variety of forms in this category ranging from a single sheet to 4-8 pages. Some will have been designed especially for this appointment (the C.S.C.* do this) and so every question is relevant. Some are so general that parts are either irrelevant or too scant. Try not to be put off by this. If this is obviously a form devised for all staff grades from school leavers to senior executives you will have to 'translate' sections to suit a person of your age, even substituting an alternative heading if necessary, e.g. some forms are not designed for graduates but the employer will really want to know what you did at your last place of full time education so substitute 'university' for 'school'. In other places there will not be enough space — as is usual in the 'jobs held' section. The simplest plan is to write it out on a separate sheet of paper following the pattern of the form. Put your name on this sheet and secure it to the form and write 'see separate sheet' in the box on the form. Another hazard with this type of form is that you suddenly find a question difficult to answer — and then discover that it isn't relevant to the post you are applying for! Look out for this if you are a non-technical man applying for a post in a very technical concern; the chief security officer, personnel manager or financial controller is not expected to know the technicalities of scientific processes.

Many companies make the application blank serve as a personnel record as well. This is confusing to applicants who find some questions suspicious or misleading. Others contain

*Civil Service Commission

questions concerned with longer term career planning — but until you know more about the structure and opportunities within the company these are impossible to answer as set. The best plan is to write 'to be discussed' for these.

Another thing to watch out for with this all-purpose form is the layout. It will probably have been designed by 'paperwork' experts with very little regard for the chap who has to provide the information, with the inevitable result that spacing is appalling and questions repetitious. This is a very real hazard if you complete the form with a typewriter as a sudden change in lay-out may be masked by the machine.

If very personal, private information is asked you are quite within your rights to withhold it at this stage but disclose it in confidence at interview; for example, you may be living with the wife of someone else in the company but don't want every little records clerk to know it. Alternatively, you can write a private note and send it sealed and marked 'personal and private' to the personnel director.

Much frustration is experienced by candidates who receive an endless succession of application blanks and so the tendency is to delay completing them or to fill them in rapidly. Neither course will help your purpose. You simply have to study each form and grit your teeth.

What do you do if the application form does not allow you to do justice to your application? This is difficult for if you ignore the form and send a full résumé you will be regarded as a maverick or as being lazy. The best plan is to complete the form as best you can and either send 2-3 sheets of additional information or attach a copy of your c.v. If you have the facilities it is a good idea to draft your application on a photocopy of the blank form first. And, of course, always draft out the answers to searching questions.

Some forms are used as a selection tool. The personnel consultants and the more sophisticated firms do this. Virtually everything asked will be highly relevant and will fall into one of the sections (a) historical information, (b) self-analytic and projective. The latter may be in narrative form or a sort of personality inventory. 'Trace the course of your career and show how well you are prepared to undertake this assignment' is a typical type of question.

These narrative questions are the most important ones that are likely to be asked and largely replace a preliminary interview. It is important when answering them to think them out very carefully, viewing them from every possible angle because, while at interview you have the opportunity fo making additional explanations and answering supplementary questions, here you have one chance only — and you don't have the benefit of seeing your inquisitor or the company premises beforehand. It may be worthwhile looking up Moodies British Companies Index if you know very little about the company as this will give you some information about staff policy and indications of the background of the directors.

All general purpose personnel forms have to be approached with caution. The early, historical part is easy enough. In the latter part every word written — or subtly avoided — will be studied. As a well-constructed application form can be a more reliable selection tool than an interview, consultants draw up a long short-list of about eight people from their study of the forms. The questions asked will probably have been researched so draft your answers with care. This does not mean that they are looking for straight conformists; far from it; what it does mean is that your voice and facial expression being absent, your words must speak for themselves. Try reading what you have written in a toneless voice to see if it affects the meaning in any way. A standard answer will not do either as your answer must reflect the job you are applying for. Incidentally, if at a later date you apply for another job through the same consultants, ask to see and, if necessary, revise your application blank as it may well contain sentiments or reflect a bias which would be totally wrong for this new appointment.

3. The psychologist's blank
This is one other type of application blank which you may have to fill in. Some companies refer all short-listed applicants for senior positions to specialist appraisal firms who will compare you with successful managers on an international scale. Or it could be that you wish to change your whole career and have decided to see a Vocational

Guidance Psychologist. You can easily identify this type of form as it is usually 'weighted' and 'scored' as you can see from the figures in the margins. It will also be more searching in its form of questioning. Much more detail will be required on such things as your academic performance by asking for the actual marks or grades you achieved in all subjects taken, and you may find it necessary to look up the original certificate. If you cannot find it the Examining Board will tell you (perhaps for a small fee) if you give them details of when and where you sat the exam. This type of form often contains a personality questionnaire and some very tricky self-portrait and self-analytic questions. Or you may be asked to complete a questionnaire or to draft a board report on a given topic or similar business exercise.

The psychologist is trying to determine what makes you 'tick'. He tries to build up a picture of you in action and within the environment of your life. He plumbs the depth and range of your knowledge and experience, the use you have made of the opportunities you have had, your behavioural pattern, your motivation, career aims and so on. And he is looking for signs of maladjustment and strain. It is difficult to complete this type of form honestly and dangerous to try to 'cheat' your way through it. The only thing to do is to answer it as fully as you can and try not to present yourself as a paragon of virtue or to let your imagination run riot. There is a strong temptation to try to be too clever in answering this type of form which must be resisted at all costs — or else you will reveal too much to your disadvantage!

A psychologist's blank may take you three hours to complete and will seem a frightful waste of time. On the other hand it enables you to give 'perfect', well-thought-out answers away from the stress of the face-to-face encounter and with your stocktaking analysis you have most of the raw material you need anyway.

Here is a *check list* to run through before you complete yet another application blank.
1. Re-read the advertisement and any other information you have received or have ascertained.
2. Make a list of the critical factors in the man

136

specification.

3. Take a photocopy of the form if you can.
4. Study the form for its content and layout.
5. Draft your answers to the tricky questions.
6. Check these against the list of critical factors; have you done full justice to yourself? If not redraft.
7. Complete the form carefully in black ink, black biro or type it (for ease of photocopying).
8. Check your answers for legibility, spelling and grammar.
9. Is there anything important you have omitted because it has not been asked? If so prepare some additional notes, refer to these on the form and attach them together firmly.
10. Check that you have signed and dated it and have your name on the additional notes.
11. Despatch it with a brief covering letter without delay (the recipient will look for dates and postmarks).
12. Have you put the job reference number on the envelope? If not, do so if it is going to a large firm or to a consultant.

9 How to make an impact in the interview

All your efforts to date in analysing the job market and in launching yourself on it with the help of skilfully prepared résumés and with leads and recommendations from agencies and friends have had one end in view; and in the first instance it is not, you may be surprised to learn, to get a job but to get an interview. That is a hurdle you will have to overcome whether you walk straight into a company chairman's office with a warm recommendation from a cabinet minister, or whether, after a long and worrying wait you have managed to get to see one of that same company's personnel officers about a post as, say, one of a team of estimating engineers on a new project. It is vitally important, therefore, that you are equipped to handle every stage of every kind of interview at every level. Never make the mistake of thinking of it as a formality, or of an initial appointment with a man at a lower level as a tiresome preliminary to the hard stuff on the short-list. You are on trial every time and each situation must be one that you negotiate cleanly and successfully.

Planning the preliminaries
Opposing generals in wartime try to find out as much as possible about the commander they are facing: his background, his education and how he fought his other battles. The man who will be on the other side of the desk to you is not your opponent, but there is an analogy here. The more you know about him and his company, the more you will be able to anticipate his questions, plan for them and answer them tellingly.

If you have gone to your library and consulted the references we set out in Appendix D (useful sources of information) you will have found out quite a lot about the company already: exactly what it does, where it operates, how many branches or subsidiaries it has, how it is expanding geographically and in terms of activities and processes, what it specialises in, how it sells its products, where it stands in relation to the competition, what progress it has made in recent years and what its problems are. If its products are on view anywhere go and look at them and try to find out discreetly what customers and retailers think of them in terms of quality, price, delivery dates and any other information that may be relevant to the kind of job you are looking for. If there is any company literature around, try to get hold of it. Maybe the firm has a showroom. An hour there might be well spent. Another good idea is to get hold of trade journals in which the company features and to keep a close eye on the business sections of the press before the interview. It is not only a question of finding out specifically about the firm's activities. At a senior level you may be asked questions about the general economic climate and intelligent opinions and background on this can be gleaned from papers such as the *Financial Times* and *The Economist*.

As mentioned previously, do your best to learn something, if possible, about the man who will interview you: this will be easy if the meeting is through an introduction from one of your important contacts. Before it takes place, get as much information as you can about what sort of people and attitudes he likes and dislikes, what aspects of the business he takes most interest in (obviously you should check up on those), what his general background is, what his personal interests are and idiosyncracies you might have to watch out for.

Unfortunately personal information like that is often hard to get, but even if you have no close acquaintances in common it may be possible to find out a good deal. If the man you are going to see is operating at the top level, you may be able to look him up in *Who's Who*; some professional bodies and institutes also publish directories of members which give at least a minimal amount of information about them. Another useful source is *British Qualifications* which will tell you exactly what the initials after his name mean and this may also give you some clue about his background and special interests. If you already know somebody in the same company it will be worthwhile having a word with him. Even if he personally doesn't have anything to do with the man you are seeing, almost invariably he will know someone who does. Most people are glad to help in this way. Another useful piece of preparation to undertake will be if the job involves travel abroad or contact with foreign customers. If you have given a language as one of your qualifications, make sure you are ready for one of the interviewers to spring a question in that language on you. Before the interview, therefore, you should refresh your knowledge of business vocabulary by reading and, ideally, by practising conversation. The international editions of *Reader's Digest* and current affairs weeklies are invaluable sources of current business terminology. A good substitute for the latter, if you have access to a tape recorder, is to use it to talk to yourself, so polishing your fluency and checking your accent.

Making your entrance

The letter you have received calling you for the interview will specify a time and, if the place is not easy to find, will probably tell you how to get there. Don't be late, under any circumstances. Most people hate to be kept waiting and are apt to regard it as both discourteous and a sign of fecklessness in the latecomer. You should give yourself plenty of time for the journey, therefore, and an allowance for the sort of thing that can go wrong — traffic jams, for instance. Remember also that if a map of the area was sent with their letter it may not be quite so clear on the ground as it looked on paper. Getting there half an hour early will give you time for a brisk, tension-relieving walk. Being ten minutes late will almost certainly mean that the odds are stacked against you before you have said a word.

Sometimes, of course, the boot will be on the other foot — you are the one who is kept waiting. But even if the time is drawing out beyond what you consider reasonable it is important to 'keep your cool'. If this happens a polite enquiry to a secretary is in order, but any sign of impatience or irritation should be avoided. These may be observed by subordinates and their opinions, both favourable and otherwise, have a habit of trickling back to superiors and may influence the impression they get of you.

Mostly, though, the interview will take place more or less on time, and any spare moments you have between arrival and being called in can be very usefully filled in by checking over your c.v. and any other papers you may have brought with you or by thinking up some further questions that may arise during the interview and how you would answer them. If you are in an ante room, trade literature, catalogues or house magazines may be laid on the table. Studying them may provide some piece of background information that may come in very useful during the interview; it may also help to relieve any tension that you may be feeling.

You and the interview

Your interviewer may be a man in the personnel management hierarchy who has been made responsible for recruitment. In other cases he may be the person you are going to work for or the divisional head to whom he is responsible. In some senior jobs you will probably meet, at some stage, a panel of interviewers who will include members of the top management. Yet another alternative — the most common one at the pre-selection stage for senior appointments — is that a firm of consultants will be handling the interview for a client to whom they will pass on the candidates whom they consider most suitable.

Like other kinds of company executives interviewers come in all shapes, sizes and abilities. Some are experienced and competent, know what they are looking for and know what sort of questions will enable them to establish whether you fill the bill. Others will leave it to you to make out a case for yourself — which is much more difficult than developing it in response to questions. If you are being interviewed by someone you will be working for directly, it will often be that, having satisfied himself about what your qualifications are and that you know what you are talking about, he will probably concentrate on the specific dimensions of the job and how you fit them. In other cases, the interviewer will be more interested in getting some kind of picture of your experience, interests and personality. Some interviewers will be polite, others — perhaps intentionally — will be awkward.

There is no stereotype for interviews, any more than there is for other kinds of human encounter. The important thing to remember is that an interview is just that. It is not an ordeal, it is not a humiliation and it is not your last chance; it is a business meeting in which you think you have something to sell and the interviewer thinks you have something to offer — otherwise he would not have asked you along.

The consultant's interview

The typical consultant's interview will take 1½ hours and follow a rather different pattern from the face-to-face meeting with a future employer. The consultant is an 'honest broker' and has to weigh the needs of both candidate and employer. His interview is therefore a two-way affair. Starting with a description of the client company and job he will give his interpretation of the scope of the appointment from the candidate's point of view. This may well take the first 20 minutes of the interview and will include some discussion and the invitation to ask questions. When it appears certain that the candidate is genuinely interested in the appointment the consultant will commence to interview usually by leading a discussion based on the needs of the company and how the candidate might set about solving them. Questions of fact will be interspersed from time to time. The discussion will then move to the career and personal needs of the candidate and to what extent this appointment will meet them.

Essentially this type of interview is a matching process and involves overt self-selection by the candidate as well as the gathering of evidence on which the consultant will eventually make his judgement. Typically the interview is a more informal and more friendly affair (but no less searching for that) than the interview with an employer — except at very senior levels when a similar approach will be adopted. After all, if the candidate is a good one the consultant will want to consider him for other jobs if this one is not entirely suitable. The difficulty with this type of interview is its permissiveness. It is very easy to be caught off your guard and the consultant being a trained and experienced interviewer is unlikely to let any weakness pass unexposed. It is also very flexible and you will be able to choose, at times, the direction that it will take, so be prepared for this. The giving of advice is a normal part of this interview so be prepared to discuss salary requirements and to seek guidance on your asking price — consultants will be very realistic about this and will often suggest that the job is revised to suit your abilities and will 'sell' you to the employer.

Handling the interview

Just as a business meeting has its course — the opening pleasantries, the sparring, the detailed negotiation and then, if it can be reached, the conclusion — so has an interview. But before dealing in detail with the kind of points that will be involved at the nitty-gritty stage there are a number of ground rules which it is useful to bear in mind.

1. Try to introduce your strong points in a subtle, unostentatious way, letting them flow out of the course of the meeting, rather than loosing them off as your opening barrage. Even if you are an executive with uncommon qualifications which have enabled you to achieve a unique record be careful how you talk about them otherwise you may be written off as a 'big head'. The facts will be in your c.v. Let that speak for itself until the appropriate occasion arises — as it will. Knowing when to say things is just as important as knowing what to say.

2. We have noted earlier that the 'passive' interviewer who lets you make all the running is particularly difficult to handle. It is easy to ramble on inconsequentially and indeed some interviewers adopt this stance deliberately inviting you to 'talk about yourself' and seeing how you handle the situation. What you should do in that case is to narrow the conversation down to something tangible. This is where your previous study of the company and its activities comes in useful. You should begin by referring to aspects of its operations which resemble work you have handled successfully and describe concisely and with specific facts what you did in a parallel situation.
    Some men find it very difficult to interview and will

give you far too much rein for comfort. If the interviewer asks 'where would you like to begin' you can ask, for example, if he would prefer that you start with your background in such and such an area, or your experience in dealing with a particular type of situation. On the other hand, some interviewers will deliberately let you choose the subject as a technique to test how well you are able to sell and to match yourself to the requirements of the job.

Don't make the mistake of asking, 'Well, where shall I start?' You have been given the opportunity to fight on ground of your own choice. Seize it by conducting that part of the interview through an emphasis on what you can do and what you have done; but remember it must always be related to what you can do for the company you want to join. Don't let your achievements sound like a business obituary. Relate the past to the future.

3. Guard against introducing too much material — irrelevant autobiographical data or details about past jobs that have no particular bearing on this one. For one thing many interviewers rightly regard a man's ability to distinguish important from less important facts as a pointer to his executive ability; for another you may only have a limited amount of time to put over your message, particularly in the earlier stages of selection when candidates are usually being seen at intervals of half an hour or so. Don't get into the position of having insufficient time to dwell on the things that will create the greatest impression.

4. Be persuasive rather than argumentative. Above all, be very careful about being drawn into an argument on matters of fact unless the point you are making is a vital one. Your interviewer may have his figures wrong on the annual tonnage of cement used in road building, but he will not relish your telling him so. You don't have to back down ignominiously, of course. Say something like, 'Well that point can be easily checked. Let's leave it open'.

5. Don't be offensive, even if you think the interviewer is. Be firm but do not lose your temper.

6. Don't name drop to make an impression — you will probably make the wrong one! However, there are times when 'who you know' is of critical importance in, for example, the consultancy world or in sales. You will sometimes be asked who you know as a measure of the level at which you are used to dealing — but beware, it may be checked out. So keep your name dropping to a minimum unless it is vital to the job.

7. Never, never run down or make snide remarks about your present or any of your previous employers, even if you think you have good cause to do so. If you are in a job but looking for a change this does not necessarily imply criticism. Say you are very happy with the firm, but that you feel the way they want your job to develop does not fit with the way you would like your career to develop — this will give you an opening to put forward some of your ideas to the interviewer. Even if you have left as a result of a blazing row there is no need to go into details unless asked to do so. If that happens explain dispassionately, briefly and unemotionally what the row was about, what your point of view was and how you differed from your colleagues. If you have become redundant as a result of a merger, or rationalisation in the wake of a fall-off in business, say no more than that; though you should have prepared a question of why your particular post was one of those singled out for redundancy.

8. If the circumstances and specifications of the job you are applying for are explained to you don't, unless invited to do so, tell the interviewer how the job should be done or express any critical opinions about how it is being done at present.

9. Don't apologise for your age. It is a common fault with the over-forty job-hunter to harp on this theme in one way or another instead of stressing his qualifications to do the job; qualifications which are enhanced and tempered by maturity, not the reverse.

First impressions

First impressions are usually important and you should try to establish a relaxed and pleasant atmosphere with your interviewer or panel of interviewers. If names are mentioned try to memorise them and use them in your answers. You will also find it useful to establish what the position in the company is of the person or persons you are seeing because, as we mentioned earlier, the kind of answers they will be looking for to get a picture of you will depend on the working relationship they expect to have of the person appointed. A man you will be working for directly will be mainly concerned with your knowledge of the ins and outs of the job. A personnel man may be more concerned with a general set of characteristics that fill the job specification he has been given, and longer term prospects with the company.

Usually the opening stages of the interview will be concerned with clarifying or expanding points in your c.v. You should now be prepared to explain the precise nature of your responsibilities in the various jobs you have held, to whom you reported, how your achievements were measured and to what extent you succeeded in meeting the objectives which had been set to you. An alert interviewer will also spot and ask about any unusual features of your career; for instance if you have ever held a job for only a short space of time, or if you made a move involving a drop (or an unusual rise) in salary. Your answers should be truthful, but if there were any points in your past where you came unstuck on a job there is no need to go into lengthy explanations or apologies about it. In any situation of this kind there are always two versions — yours and the other man's — and if you feel your side of the story is the right one, go ahead and give it. You could say, for instance, 'I didn't feel, after a while, that I was quite getting the chance to develop my ideas at ABC Ltd that I'd hoped for, so when I got an offer from XYZ I decided to take it'. Having said that, of course, you should be prepared to answer questions on what exactly some of those ideas were.

The problem question

Having satisfied himself on the basic facts of your career the interviewer can now get on to establishing how well you are likely to be able to do the job he is hoping to fill. One good way to do this is to put to you a number of problems that either actually cropped up in the job or that are analogous to it. He may take up a point in your c.v. and say:

1. Our Australian agents have a contract with us that has another two years to run, but we're not very happy about their performance. How would you handle that one?'

2. 'I see that at XYZ you achieved 15% increase in productivity by improving labour relations. What sort of problems did you have to cope with? How did you solve them? What did you do first?'

3. 'We have just produced such and such a product. Here it is. We're rather disappointed with the way it's going. Have you any ideas on why it's doing badly? What would you do about it?'

4. 'Let's take the following situation: a manufacturer of lawn mowers is getting complaints from his customers that it's taking too long to get spares. The wholesalers say that it's uneconomic to keep a full range of spares and that it's the manufacturer's fault for taking too long to deliver. How would you solve the problem?'

5. 'Due to expansion we're thinking of moving our factory away from here. What sort of location would you move it to, and what would be your reasons for making that choice?'

6. 'In the instance above what are the main steps that have to be undertaken, and what would be your priorities in tackling them?'

7. 'One of our plants has a very much higher labour turnover than our average. How would you set about looking into the reasons for this?'

8. 'We're finding it very difficult to get skilled labour for such and such an operation. What can we do about it?'

9. 'You've got some very interesting ideas, but they would obviously cost money to implement. Have you any idea what the scale of expenditure would be? And over what period could we expect to recover our investment?'

10. 'If we were to offer you the job, how would you set

about seeing what sort of things have to be done right away?'

The possibilities for this sort of question are obviously endless and it would be impossible to prepare in specific terms for their content. However, these instances do illustrate in a general way, the principles underlying them. What the interviewer wants to establish is your judgement, your ability to express yourself and be decisive and constructive in solving problems. A mature and experienced executive need have no apprehension about this stage of the interview. He will have come up against precisely such situations in the course of his career, and dealt with them. Indeed in this very fact there is a pitfall to be avoided. A tendency to talk too much is a common failing as men approach middle age. Typically such men have seen and done a lot and therefore have a lot more to talk about. This can be very interesting at the right time and place, but not now. What you have to do is to get to the point fast and stick to it. Avoid reminiscences, and if you have to relate some anecdote from a previous job keep it short and keep it relevant. Use your experience, but do not spell it out in detail.

Will your face fit?

Having assessed your ability to handle the techniques of the post the interviewer will then move to some more general aspects. In particular he will be interested in establishing how you will be likely to fit in as a person. Consequently he will ask personal questions and you have to realise that this is part of his job, even if he is a personnel man who may be junior to you in years and a good deal down the ladder in terms of your previous jobs. It is his business to build up a picture of your stability, your health, your ability to get on with superiors and subordinates, your interests outside the job, what sort of books, newspapers and periodicals you read, your attitude to foreigners and to coloured people; maybe even the sort of friends you have. He will have an eye both on whether you are likely to get along with your colleagues, and the fact that as an executive you will probably be in the position of meeting people outside the firm as its representative. A firm's representatives, you will appreciate, are not just its salesmen; every senior member of the company creates to the outside world an image of what that company is and stands for. As far as your personality in relation to the job is concerned, he may also ask you what you feel your strongest (and maybe weakest) traits as an executive are and what aspects of the job you feel you will like doing best. You should think carefully, before the interview, how you will handle a question of this nature. It is almost as important as another awkward one that often comes up with the mature executive applying for a job slightly lower down the ladder from his previous one and can be phrased something like this: 'Aren't you "over-qualified" or "too experienced" for this job?'

Even if this question is not voiced you may sense that it is being implied in the interviewer's attitude to you. In these cases you should find an appropriate opportunity to stress that an executive with your experience needs much less time in which to get to grips with the job. It is a common complaint of employers that a new man is not really earning his keep for the first six months because it takes that long to pick up the threads of what is involved. Like everyone else, you will need time to get acclimatised, but in your case it will take *less* time. As for being over-qualified, you might tactfully point out that in a job and a company which is growing all the time it is an advantage to have a man who has more qualifications than are needed, just as the same company, planning a factory or a warehouse, would build for its needs *ahead* of its present level of business.

Negotiating the salary
Obviously salary is another question you should be prepared to deal with; particularly as it can be said to have two dimensions — the actual salary level you expect and the point in the interview at which the issue is raised.

Where you have replied to an advertisement usually the salary is stated, either in precise terms or as falling in a certain range. In other instances the salary profile may be more vague: 'not less than £ . . .' or 'a suitable applicant will be unlikely to be earning less than £ . . .' or 'salary will be negotiable in the region of £ . . .'. In all those cases the salary level will be a matter for discussion at the interview; and, of course, it will be of prime importance where you have been asked to attend an interview in reply to an on spec letter or some other initiative from you.

The greatest difficulty is when the question of salary comes up early in the interview, before you have had time to get an idea of the scope and responsibilities of the position and the opportunity for advancement. Until those details have been clarified any proposals you might make would be based on little more than your desire for a certain sum of money. You should, of course, have decided prior to the interview what your salary aims are and what is the least you will work for — the considerations to take into account are outlined in chapter 4. But until you know a good deal about what the job involves you are not in possession of the facts that will enable you to negotiate the right kind of figure. Thus, if you are invited to discuss salary matters early on in the interview it may be advisable to suggest diplomatically that more details about the position and your qualifications to fill it should be gone into first, so that you can get a better idea of what you can do for the company.

The interviewer will seldom have a hard and fast figure in mind — but usually he will have decided, or had outlined to him, the maximum the company is willing to pay for the particular job that is being offered. However, if he can get a good man at a bargain price he is unlikely to let the opportunity slip. To that extent, and within certain limits, how good a deal you get is up to you. So what is the best way to handle the situation?

Generally, it will be left to you to initiate the salary question. You should phrase your question by talking about a *starting* figure, thereby implying that you expect your performance to be worth more to the company when you have worked your way into the job. Another approach is to ask what salary range the company has in mind. The use of the word 'range' implies that, although you do not insist on starting at the top if there is room for the job to grow, you do expect your remuneration to increase once you have shown your ability to produce results. Indeed, in general it is a good idea to centre the discussion on future prospects. You might say, once the job has been outlined to you, 'That sounds like a position that will be worth £6,000 in two or three years' time. That could be a very exciting opportunity, so I'll be happy to leave it to you to determine the starting figure'. Such an approach labels you as a £6,000 a year man who can be obtained for a lower figure now. It also enables you to name a figure which is close to your actual expectations but which, mentioned as a starting salary, might frighten the interviewer off. Even if he thinks you are worth it, it might, for instance, be too much out of line with what he is paying people for similar jobs at present.

This same tactic is a useful one in the tricky situation where you are applying for a job which actually carries a lower remuneration than the one you have been earning. Managers tend to be suspicious of a man who is ready to take a drop in salary and in that situation you might say, 'Well that sounds like something that would put me on about my present level in a couple of years' time. Obviously, I appreciate it'll be a case of working myself into a new job, so there'll be an initial cut involved, but it sounds such an exciting job that I'm willing to take a chance on that.'

Tact is essential at this stage of the discussion. It is unwise to attempt to bargain. You may know your worth; but for the company that is considering you, you are an unknown quantity. The time to raise your sights is when this is no longer the case. On the other hand it is disastrous to imply, as you may be tempted to do if the job-hunting process is not going well, that you might be willing to take the job at less than the advertised salary 'until you have proved your value' or some such phrase. This will not get you the job and it may undermine your morale.

The questions you should ask

As the interview draws to the final stages, you will probably be asked whether you have any questions — whether all the points you might want to know about have been covered.

It is wise and tactful to begin by asking about matters which show your interest in the work — what you can do for the company rather than what the company might do for you. Thus you might start by asking if there is any way you could prepare yourself for the job if it was offered to you; for instance if there is any company literature or job manuals which are available for you to look through. You might also ascertain if there have been any special problems or difficulties which are likely to crop up in the job and which you could think over ways and means of tackling. Apart from anything else this might give you a pointer as to why the previous incumbent of the job no longer has it. The attitude of the interviewer towards your predecessor could be a significant factor when you come to make a decision as to whether or not you can work with him.

If you are going to have staff working under you, this stage of the interview is a good opportunity to get to know about them — what their age and experience is, and in what ways they are most likely to need and respond to your leadership.

Another point worth touching on is whether the company provides any facilities for further executive training in the way of internal or external management courses. For instance, you might say, 'If this job develops in the way you've outlined it, I imagine it will be necessary for me to get some further grounding in financial management. What sort of opportunities will there be, apart from private study, to get more into the subject?'

Of course, this does not mean to say that important matters regarding personal benefits should be left open. While it is not advisable for an executive to ask about hours you do need to find out how much evening and weekend time you will be expected to devote to company affairs.

Other points that you will want to check, however, are:

1. Whether there is a contract of service and what its provisions are. For instance, there might be a clause preventing you from undertaking any outside paid work. If you are, say, receiving an income from writing articles for a professional journal it is important to make a decision whether to give up this work, clear it with your future employer, or not to take the job.

2. Whether there is a company pension scheme, when you become eligible for it, and whether it is contributory or non-contributory.

3. Whether, in addition to the stated salary, there are any

commissions, bonuses or profit-sharing schemes.

4. If the job involves travelling or entertaining, whether expenses are payable as incurred, or on a fixed allowance; and if the latter, how much it is.
5. Is a company car provided?
6. If the job involves moving abroad or to another part of the country, is any assistance given with removal expenses?
7. When would it be convenient for the company to have you start work?
8. Will it be possible (in the case of small firms) to acquire a share of the equity?

When you have satisfied yourself on these points — and you should be careful to keep to essentials and not to drag out your part of the questioning process for too long — indicate that you have finished. Don't just lapse into silence, but say something like, 'Thank you. I don't think I have any more questions'.

Some basic interview etiquette

If you have not been used to interviews and are more accustomed to the casual relationship of executive equals it is useful to bear in mind some of the rules of the more formal relationship that governs an interview. The following are some elementary but important points of etiquette.

1. Don't sit down immediately you enter the room. If the interviewer does not ask you to be seated let a moment elapse before you do so.
2. Don't walk into the room smoking and do not 'light up' unless invited to do so.
3. Even if you are nervous, try not to betray the fact by irritating mannerisms such as rubbing your hands, fiddling with a pen and so forth.
4. Look at the interviewer unless he is interrupted by a subordinate or a telephone call. In that case it is polite to glance away.

After the interview

At the end of the interview you may have been given a hint about whether or not you are likely to be offered the job.

Perhaps you will have sensed yourself that things have gone your way and that you are in with a chance — or not. Or you may be told that you will have to meet yet another executive before a final decision is made (it is common practice at senior levels to meet the chairman and the Board — usually on an informal basis). If so, do make sure that anything you slipped up on at interview will be well covered next time and if you have any areas of doubt note them down and either check them out or make sure that you find out the answer when you next meet.

But however well the interview went, don't assume that the job is 'in the bag' until you have a firm offer in writing. No news is not necessarily good news because firms may take weeks to make up their minds before turning you down 'with regret'. So don't stop your job search until things are safely tied up; hard experience shows that the chances are 4:1 against you, even if you do reach the short-list stage.

So now you have done everything you possibly can to get this particular job and you are waiting anxiously for the mail. Perhaps you will have had several irons in the fire simultaneously and, since when one's luck changes it is apt to do so dramatically, you may suddenly find yourself in the position of having more than one job offer. If this is the case you will have to weigh up the longer term prospects, the considerations of job satisfaction, the reputation of your potential employers as a business and in their attitude towards their staff, the working surroundings, whether you are likely to find your colleagues congenial, and the comparative salaries and benefits of each job. There are a lot of factors to think about and it is right that you should make your decision carefully. But if you are in this position, and want a few days to think matters over, you should inform the parties concerned — don't lapse into a puzzling silence.

Don't leave such a decision open for more than a week at the outside and, having made up your mind, inform the firm you are turning down that you have decided to accept another offer. Once again, this is not only good manners, but good sense. Having spotted you as a promising executive they might at some future point approach you about something even better.

10 Other methods you might encounter

Because it is recognised that interviews are an imperfect selection tool, some employers adopt other methods or reply on the advice of an outside 'expert' — hence the rise of the management selection consultant! What other methods of selection are you likely to have to face? There are five main ones and one occasional one:

> psychological tests
> depth interviews
> group interviews
> behavioural exercises
> selection boards
> meet the wife.

Psychological tests
There are three main types:

> General aptitude
> Special aptitude
> Personality

As you could be faced by all three we will describe all of them briefly.

General aptitude
General aptitude tests set out to measure the extent to which you can solve new problems, your mental flexibility in seeking and finding solutions to problems. For some jobs this is important especially if there will be a lot of entirely new material to learn. For the older applicant untimed, power tests are usually used. You are unlikely to finish one of these as they become progressively more and more difficult. You vocabulary and your ability to perceive abstruse sequences are the principal measures used.

Special aptitude
These measure your reasoning ability with a certain type of

material — words, mechanisms, figures, letter/number sequences. They are correlated with a special type of skill such as those employed in abstract reasoning, editing, engineering, accountancy, computer skills and so on. In some cases they assume some previous knowledge and the tester will attempt to assess this separately. Special aptitude tests are mostly used when the individual will have to use a latent skill or develop one in a new job. You are more likely to meet one if you want to change your type of job radically than if you want to continue in your old line.

Personality
There are two types of personality test — projective and behavioural. The projective type, of which the Rorschach Ink Blot test is the best known, asks you to describe the feelings or emotions that are aroused in you by an abstract shape. Responses tend to follow set patterns and the extent to which the candidate's reactions follow one pattern or another is scored. As with all personality tests there is no right or wrong answer; the tester is concerned with the emotional make up of the candidate and from this is able, by reference to research studies and to his knowledge of human behaviour, to predict future behaviour.

The behavioural tests — 16 PF and the MMPI are the most used — ask the candidate to say how he tends to behave in a number of typical situations. In every case he is forced to choose which action he is most likely to take. Now anyone can deliberately give the answers he thinks the tester wants — but the tester is quite up to this one and will automatically examine the result for an 'ideal' or a 'true' response. After all no sensible tester will use one measuring instrument in isolation and it is the overall fit of all the evidence that he is concerned with. A faked test score tells him something about the candidate — but it may not be to the candidate's advantage! The tester enters all scores onto a profile and will usually weight them statistically to compare them with the norm (if he has occupational norms) or with a population — such as industrial managers. As this type of test gives a behavioural pattern, i.e. it shows how the candidate tends to behave (or would like the tester to believe he would behave) in certain types of situation, it is relatively easy for him to predict future behaviour in a new job (because people behave more predictably than they think they do).

We have dealt with this subject at some length as more and more companies are using tests as part of their selection procedures and to many readers they may be a largely unknown quantity.

Depth interviews

If you are referred to a consultant for a second opinion he will give you a 'depth interview'. By this we mean an interview lasting around 1½ hours in which you will be asked to think pretty deeply about your work, your life, your motives, goals, philosophy of management etc. The consultant will be interested in your total existence and in the use you have made of the opportunities you have had in life. Some of this will seem at the time to be of little relevance and many will ask you to recall things you have not thought about for years. Some interviewers will attempt to 'stress' you (they shouldn't as this makes the interview even less valid!) and by putting pressure on you hope to force you to show your true self. This is tedious but if you start to pin him back by asking him stressful questions (i.e. 'How do you justify the existence of a department of this size when the company's profit record is so poor?' — and if you've done your homework you will probably have more facts and figures at your finger tips than he has) it usually lowers the temperature very rapidly! If you have followed faithfully all the steps in chapter 3 you will be well prepared for this type of interview and will not only take it in your stride but also do yourself full justice.

Depth interviewing is often accompanied by psychological testing and the test indications are discussed with the candidate.

Group interviews or meet the board

Provided that you are well prepared for them group interviews can be quite fun! If not they can be confusing and rather terrifying. The usual practice is for each member of the panel to discuss one topic in turn while the others listen, assess and take notes. Five or six pairs of eyes fastened upon your every movement and facial twitch is unnerving at first — unless you are an exhibitionist in which case it is nice to be the centre of attention. The thing to do is to notice their reactions and facial expressions, assess them, and then play up to them! This is not as difficult as it might sound. They are not on their guard as you are. You will soon find their favourite topic and you can feed them with tit-bits from time to time. This may sound facetious but it really can be done because as a selection technique board interviews are cumbersome and do not allow that depth of rapport which is the characteristic of the good man-to-man interview. The same is equally true when you have the chance to meet the board. Unless you are very sure of yourself and wish to make a rapid make or break appeal it will pay you to box carefully and play safe until you have had the chance to assess the general climate and the balance of power. You should then make sure that the most influential member of the board (you will probably be asked to sit next to or opposite him at lunch) has a good chance of assessing you fairly and that his questions are answered properly — at the expense of others if need be (you will soon learn whom you can politely ignore). It is always dangerous to cross swords on these occasions; far better to compromise and seek out your adversary later if you decide to join them. For this is very much a two-way exercise to see how well you would fit in with each of them and become a full member of the team. From that point of view it is most useful and you should take full advantage of the opportunity given you. You will also be able to assess them as your future colleagues and friends and get a clearer idea of the unique contribution you will be able to make and what experience you will be able to gain as part of this team.

Behavioural exercises

All the short-listed candidates are seated around a table and are given a group exercise to tackle. The assessors are seated around the periphery or take a minor part in the proceedings. They are interested in observing how each individual sets about influencing the others and the role he tends to take and how well he is accepted by the others. In some cases roles are assigned; in others they have to be agreed or fought for! Often two exercises are set: one, a short, sociological one, will be based on the discussion of a controversial topic which may have little direct relevance to the appointment or to the company. The other will be task oriented. Roles will probably be assigned and switched at intervals. Usually you will all be members of a working party with a highly relevant, work-related task to perform — such as devising or giving your considered opinion upon a policy matter. You will be fed the data you need or ask for.

This method of selection was very much in vogue during the '50s and early '60s but is not so widely used today. It has the advantage that you are all seen in action and in interaction; but it is a difficult exercise to assess, is brutal and tends to favour certain types of people and to show others in an unfavourable light. All these situations are perforce contrived and the whole thing can fall horribly flat. However, forewarned is forearmed, so be prepared!

Selection boards

Basically, this is a combination of tests, interviews and activities designed to provide a wide range of information about you, your personality and your abilities. It is used by many of the larger companies as well as by the Armed Services and the Civil Service. Sometimes it is the precursor to a final 'depth' interview and then must be regarded as a winnowing process before the final decision is made.

Naturally, the procedure varies considerably, but it is a very thorough method of assessment. Candidates are under observation for a far longer time than is possible by most other means of selection and they can be put through a larger variety of tests. To say that there is a fool-proof way to succeed would be ridiculous, but there is a definite advantage in having some idea of what to expect. There are also a few sensible preparations you can make to ensure that you show yourself to your best advantage.

The Selection Board normally takes two days and there can be anything up to eight candidates on any Board. It is normally stressed that it is not a competition and that it is theoretically possible for everybody in the group to pass or fail. As part of the point of the Board is in seeing a man in contrast to others, it is inevitable that a competitive element creeps in. There is no real harm in this if it helps you to keep yourself mentally sharp.

There are usually three main activities on a Board: written tests, verbal group activity and interviews.

1. Written tests

One of the earliest of these is a personal assessment, which can be tricky if it takes you by surprise. You are presented with a blank sheet on which is written a question like, 'Write a description of yourself as seen by a friend'. Either together with this, or, in some cases when you have finished it, you get another sheet which says 'Describe yourself as seen by a critic'. There is nothing sinister about either of these questions, but as you will have only a limited time in which to answer, it helps a great deal to give some thought to them before and at leisure. What you are prepared to say about yourself is your own affair, but it is as well not to be too extravagant and above all keep the two answers balanced; otherwise you may end up with an extremely hostile friend and an unusually tolerant critic. Try writing a specimen paragraph for each of these; then check it against what previous work reports may have said about you. An understanding wife or a frank friend can be a great help to see that the accounts are neither too idealistic nor too humble.

Other tests are usually of the more conventional intelligence test type. These usually measure verbal, numerical and visuo-spatial ability. It is not possible to do very much about one's I.Q., but you will find that with a little practice you can improve your score at these sorts of tests. Try several equal tests one after another, and in between, have a thorough post-mortem on your mistakes. You should find that, once you get into the swing of it, your performance will be improved considerably on your first 'cold' effort. (You can obtain books containing these tests quite easily in paperback form, one good source being *Test Your Own I.Q.* by H.J. Eysenck, published by Pelican.)

Quite often there are general knowledge questions,

usually with a heavy current affairs bias. These tend to concentrate on the names of people in the international news scene, so time spent browsing through an international *Who's Who* should pay off. Certainly you should read one of the serious newspapers thoroughly for some time before the Board.

Your final written work will be in the form of a major project or problem. You are presented with a bulky file of assorted information about a particular problem, which may or may not be connected with the body holding the Selection Board. This usually devolves around the siting of a major factory or installation at several alternative sites, each with its own advantages and drawbacks. There is really no prior preparation you can do for this. There is usually no one answer which is the correct one. You are being tested on your ability to assess and solve a difficult problem. Write down the possible courses of action and the factors affecting each one; then make your choice and say clearly why you prefer it to the other courses available to you. But remember that you are often working against time, allow yourself time to write down your answer whatever it is. At a later stage you may also be asked to draft a letter or a reply dealing with a specific problem, to test your ability to express yourself clearly and in some problems, tactfully.

2. Verbal group activity
This is the main area in which you will be compared in action with the other candidates on the Board. You may be asked to discuss, without a chairman, a matter of current interest, and later to discuss other matters with each of the group taking it in turn to lead. These latter discussions are often connected with facets of the main written problem. You will be assessed from three aspects. What qualities do you exhibit in an unchaired discussion; are you dominant or passive and above all constructive? Secondly, when working in committee under a Chairman, can you contribute as part of a directed team? Finally, if you are in charge, can you communicate the problem clearly to your group and are you able to get the best out of the group's combined abilities?

3. Interviews

At a Selection Board there are usually at least three members or assessors. They will be headed by a chairman, who is usually part of the personnel function of the body holding the Board. One of the other members is usually trained in psychology and will be concentrating mainly on your motivation and background. The other one is usually a senior serving member of the branch, department or service which is doing the recruiting. He will primarily be concerned with your suitability for a job rather than the more general approach of the others. You will normally have an interview with each one of the assessors. Sometimes you may have to provide a list of topics you are willing to discuss in some depth. Here, you should avoid subjects which are too narrowly specialised, but they should be things you can talk about sensibly and with a definite viewpoint. This again is an area where a little sensible preparation can improve your performance.

In general you should, unless you are an introvert, enjoy the Selection Board. A sense of comradeship does develop among candidates. It is worth listening to the comments the others make about an interviewer you have yet to see. If you do not perform well at one test, remember that results are considered on all the tests and that some are more important than others. Finally, though a Selection Board is by no means a perfect method of selecting an individual for a job, it is certainly one of the most thorough, and does give you a chance, especially if you are changing your field to be selected for what you are, rather than for what you may or may not have done in the past.

Meet the wife

This is popular in the U.S.A. and is used in Britain where a man's wife will be actively involved in his work or where the effect on the man's family will be considerable — such as prolonged absence from home, a job abroad, social work where a man's home will be used, or a board appointment where the man will need to have an accomplished hostess for a wife. People in Britain do not care much for this idea but if one thinks about it, in some appointments, a man's wife may be a great asset or a major liability.

How then are wives assessed? Two popular methods are used and both of them are only semi-formal. The most usual is a dinner engagement where the candidate's wife is invited to be the hostess. The chairman may, in effect, invite himself to dinner (he will probably provide the champagne). He will expect no more than a normal, semi-informal, friendly dinner party and this gives your wife a chance to ask questions as well.

The other method is to invite wives to come to discuss any problems they foresee and generally to ask questions. The major overseas companies provide this service partly to save time (a trained secretary who has been to the country can often answer the questions better than a busy executive and with less strain) and partly out of self-interest; a dissatisfied wife is often the major cause of high staff turnover in overseas assignments − and of course the obverse is equally true.

So your wife need have nothing to fear. In many cases she will have a very enjoyable night out − and it will be you who will be on tenterhooks hoping that you have briefed her sufficiently in case she gets the names or companies mixed.

11 How to wait sensibly - and maybe profitably

Studying the press, attending interviews, writing letters, drafting c.v.s and filling up application blanks — all the paraphernalia of looking for a job — is a time-consuming business, and there are indeed those who advocate that it should be a full-time occupation. Whether or not a man is happy to devote all his energies to it is a matter of temperament; and whether he can afford to do so may ultimately boil down to a matter of finance. But many executives, for whom their working life has been a major interest, find the lack of a positive activity while they are waiting for the right job to come up a major problem in itself. The danger that also has to be watched, particularly over a longer period, is simply that of getting out of the habit of working. It is important to keep as mentally active and up-to-date as you were when you were employed, and there are many ways to do this. In some cases, furthermore, they may present the opportunity to bring some extra money rolling in.

Most readers of this book will have thought about the possibility of paid part-time work and will be familiar with the numerous advertisements offering lucrative-sounding opportunities in this sphere. Some of these are perfectly above-board, though they generally involve selling extremely hard a product that is intrinsically hard to sell — no instances, no pack drill. Very often, too, the suggestion is that you should try to sell to your friends. Selling a friend something he does not much want to buy is a good way of spoiling a relationship and, as we have suggested in an earlier chapter, your personal contacts are much too useful to you in the job-hunting process to be used in this peripheral way.

One must also say that some of these part-time opportunities should be approached with great caution. In any situation where men are forced to look around for a source of income and have some capital available, as is the case with many redundant executives, thére are sharks ready to come out of the rocks. If, therefore, any proposal that is being put to you involves your own money into it, it is absolutely vital that you investigate it as thoroughly as possible.

Consult your bank manager, accountant and solicitor (cautious individuals though they may be). They are able to render invaluable service if only in terms of formulating your doubts or asking you to face up to and answer those nagging questions that your enthusiasm has pushed to the back of your mind. The opinion of well-informed City friends will be worth having — even if they have no direct information themselves they may know merchant bankers or business journalists who can provide it. You yourself should also check some of the sources set out in Appendix D. Broadly speaking, however, it would not be going too far to say that you should not commit money to somebody else's venture unless you know the people concerned personally or receive a favourable report on them from more than one person whose judgement and integrity you have cause to trust.

Not all the opportunities for keeping yourself constructively occupied are in business; nor do they all produce a direct financial reward. But no doubt most people will think first of all of the ways to augment their income, so let us begin by looking at the area of short-term and part-time employment. First of all some general principles.

Whatever you decide to go for, your aim should still be to remain very much in the hunt for a permanent job. So, if you are taking an assignment in your own field, and you are aiming to return to it, you would be unwise to take on anything which is too far below the level at which you have been used to working. Apart from the fact that it is bad for morale, it might not look good if it came out in an interview. The next point is that if what you are being offered is something that involves regular working hours and it is going to run for more than a couple of weeks, you should make it clear that you are going to need a reasonable and clear-cut arrangement of time off for interviews: something like one day out in ten, when needed and without payment, might be the sort of basis you could discuss. A third factor to bear in

165

mind is that you should not make a commitment that binds you morally or legally to an extended period of notice.

Very few temporary jobs for executives are ever advertised, but this fact in itself gives a clue to the direction your search should take. The point is that the availability of such work is sporadic and unpredictable: a man falls ill in the middle of a specialist assignment; a report suddenly needs writing in a hurry; an unexpected contract creates a temporary personnel problem; a salesman in a key territory is laid up after a car accident. Circumstances such as these can all create a situation where a man offering his services as a stand-in would be welcomed with open arms. But if such a job were advertised, by the time a suitable person was found the need for him would have gone. Therefore, and though there are a few agencies for temporary executive assignments, getting a job of this kind depends very much on your initiative and on being in the right place at the right time.

In an ad hoc situation like this, it is obviously difficult to lay down any hard and fast strategy to adopt. Rather, we would like to suggest some general avenues of approach.

1. Put the word around
When you are talking to friends and contacts about a permanent job, mention also that you are available for short-term assignments. Certain skills, of course, are more in demand than others. For instance, business has a considerable appetite for the analysis of financial and marketing information and a smaller firm may not want to go to the expense of bringing in a fully fledged consultant for this purpose. In such cases an accountant or a numerate marketing man might well fill the bill. Personnel and training problems are also an area where management might look to the help of a skilled outsider, either by preparing a report to form a basis for company action, or by tackling a specific problem such as selecting candidates for supervisory or junior executive jobs.

2. Advertise your availability
Line advertisements in trade and specialist journals are not expensive. Analyse your skills and consider which of them

would be of most interest to a firm looking for temporary executive help. Very likely this would not be in an area involving general decision-making which requires an inside knowledge of the firm concerned, but in tackling short-term, specialist problems. A sales executive from the printing industry, for instance, might phrase his advertisement like this:

> Thinking of selling print to industry? I can prepare a comprehensive report on new opportunities, problems and make specific suggestions on how and where to get business — based on ten years' experience in the field and a wide range of contacts with purchasing decision-taking executives. Ring . . . for further details.

As is the case with your main job search, the emphasis must be on specific assets you have to offer, and should embody suggestions on how they can be used by the person you are trying to reach. Approaches like, 'Redundant sales director, early forties, extensive contacts. Any offers?' — and one sees plenty of variations of this theme around — are simply a waste of money.

3. Use your overseas contacts
Your overseas business friends will not be able to help you in the same direct way as those you have at home, but it is worth suggesting to them that you may be available for a short-term assignment in case anybody they know in your field is interested in getting a detailed survey of opportunities in this country. A foreign businessman contemplating an exploratory visit over here could save himself a great deal of time if he comes primed with such information as where to locate his factory, what the labour market is like in a particular area and generally what sort of decisions he is likely to have to take. Once again, you should not only say that you are available, but should also make specific suggestions about the kind of service that you could undertake.

4. Check the agencies

There are a few agencies and other bodies that sometimes have short-term executive assignments on their books.

Executive Aide Register
114 Station Road
Oxted, Surrey
Have assignments for managers running from a few days to six months. Applicants must have been earning over £3,000. Write enclosing c.v.

Executemps
21-22 Poland Street
London W1
Specialists in providing jobs for both partly and fully qualified temporary accountants.

International Executives S.A.R.L.
Re-locating offices from Grayshott, Surrey
to Central London
Markets short- and long-term assignments for senior executives, mainly in the 45-65 group who have been earning £4,000-£5,000. These may occur abroad.

Institute of Personnel Management
5 Winsley Street
London W1
A register of temporary opportunities, for members only, is maintained by Miss F. Neale, the appointments registrar. Apply in writing.

Mr. G.M. Stephens
1414 Warwick Road
Knowle, Solihull
Mr. Stephens is the Honorary Registrar of a temporary job service for the Engineers Guild. Though intended mainly for retired men it occasionally has openings for other applicants. They must be members of one of the engineering institutions.

5. Communicate your expertise

Communication is a growth industry. In a world of rapid change there is a tremendous appetite for information about new technologies and techniques, new economic and social developments and new methods of doing old tasks more efficiently. On the other hand there is a shortage of people who have the gift, the background and the time to communicate this knowledge effectively. If you have specialist qualifications and up-to-date experience you should, therefore, consider lecturing possibilities. Get in touch with consultancy firms offering lectures and seminars in your area of expertise. Professional institutes are often glad to add a good lecturer to their list if they run regular courses. They are also frequently approached about lecturers by outside bodies. Another approach worth making in this context is to the staff training centres of large firms and to the principals of any Colleges of Further Education in your area.

A further sector of the information market where the demand exceeds the supply is in writing. We are not here talking about novels or books for the general reader — where the rewards, except for a tiny minority, are exceedingly meagre — but of technical books and articles. There are about 300 specialist, professional and technical magazines in Britain, the main ones being listed in *British Rate and Data* or *Writers' and Artists' Yearbook*. The editors of these are nearly always glad to be able to use an outside contributor who both knows his subject and can write good, readable prose. Rates vary greatly but average around £12 per thousand words.

Book publishers are also glad to hear from prospective authors in such fields as management, technology, science and accountancy. The best approach here is to write to an appropriate publisher sending an outline of the subject matter you propose to cover, a specimen chapter, a note of what sort of audience the book is aimed at, any competing titles that you know to exist (and why your book is going to be better and different!) and any other relevant details, such as your qualifications as an author. If you have no idea which publisher handles which types of books ask your local librarian or look round the shelves of any large bookshop. Publishers normally pay authors a royalty on the published price of the book — for a first work in hardback this will usually be 10%. If he is obviously very keen to do the book you may also be able to persuade him to give you an advance against royalties when you sign the contract.

Keeping yourself up-to-date
Whether or not your book is accepted for publication eventually, the mere effort of writing it will have two useful spin-offs: it will keep you busy and it will keep you up-to-date with your subject. Both are important whatever you may be doing. You should keep in touch with all the developments that are going on in your industry even when you are not employed in it. Make a regular trip to a good reference library to read the journals and other important new publications.

Another good way to keep in touch — and to fill gaps in your knowledge — is to attend courses. This will cost you money but it could be a good investment, not only for when you get a job, but in terms of talking more knowledgeably in interviews. The Institute of Directors particularly recommended their intensive 2½ day AGL (Automated Group Learning) courses. Particulars are obtainable from the Institute.

A recent and particularly welcome development is the creation of the Government Vocational Training Scheme under which unemployed persons on the Department of Employment Professional and Executive Register may apply for financial assistance towards further training. The kind of course that would be eligible for such assistance would be full-time, short, intensive ones in areas like work study, management, O & M, personnel management or (where employment in the export field is being sought) foreign languages. College fees are paid together with an allowance during training, particulars of which are given in a leaflet, PL 394, issued by the D.E. Special courses are not normally set up — applicants join current college courses.

12   New Horizons

When you have completed your self-analysis you may have come to the conclusion that you should try to build a career in another area or apply your expertise in another way. Or it may be that after looking around for a certain type of job without success for several months you are searching in other areas for possible openings; or you may have a hankering for setting up in business on your own. Whatever the reason it is well worth while considering such possibilities – if only to get it out of your system!

The business of building a new career is a vast topic and would need another book to itself if we were to cover it adequately; but let us look at the main possibilities.

Self employment

Not everyone has the qualities of an entrepreneur – a sharp eye for a commercial opening, a willingness to take risks, a readiness to accept all the responsibility going and to work long hours as well – but they are essential to succeed in business on your own.

Self employment can be broken down into three main categories:

> providing a service
> running a business
> creative, manufacturing enterprise

The inadequacies of language do not permit us to make the fine distinction we would like so let us explain what we mean.

A *service* is essentially helping people out in this context. For example, a staff agency, a hedge- and lawn-cutting service, kennels and that sort of thing; it includes professional services such as consultancy, insurance, etc.

A *business* is where you are buying and selling, running a shop or an hotel or pub, or running a franchise. It also

171

includes having riding stables, farming, nursery gardening etc.

Creative, manufacturing enterprise is where you are turning a creative talent such as cabinet making or the marketing of some gadget you have invented into a livelihood.

Whatever appeals to you there are several essential steps to take before you start to look for premises, to attempt to raise money, or commit yourself in any way.

1. *Examine the literature.*

   There are many books available from the larger libraries that will tell you how to set about it, how to keep records and explaining the technicalities of the job. For example, if you decide to start an antique business there are books on furniture, on jewelry, on porcelain, silver, brass etc. It is one thing to dabble as an amateur but if you intend to set up in business you need to become an expert which means knowing how things are made, priced and restored, how to recognise fakes etc. Take the trade journal.

2. *Talk to people in the business.*

   Most people are only too glad to give their advice to someone starting up. By talking to people in the trade you soon get a feel of the business and what the pitfalls are. Go to exhibitions and fairs or — still taking antiques as an example — visit country mansions and museums to see as much of the good stuff as you can.

3. *Get professional advice*

   Much advice is available at little or no cost. Talk to your bank manager, to your accountant, to your local chamber of commerce (they will tell you about local trading conditions and may be able to give you some introductions). These are shrewd men who take a broad, objective view and whose advice and suggested lines of enquiry should be heeded, as they will almost certainly save you time, money and frustration.

4. *Attend a course.*

   There are courses available for almost any subject that you can think of. Your local College of Further Education or reference library will advice you where you can go for what. If you are a member of B.I.M. some

evaluation of these courses is available.

Franchising

Taking up a franchise is a method of setting up in business on your own which has attracted a good deal of attention in recent years: Wimpy Bars, Golden Egg Restaurants and Arnold Palmer golf ranges are three familiar examples of franchising operations. Essentially a franchise is a form of licence which entitles a company or an individual investor to use the name and methods of a parent organisation in making available a product or service. The licence will include: (a) an obligation on the parent to provide continuing assistance in such areas as publicity and management guidance in return for a fee which may be a share of the profits, a royalty on gross turnover or a mark-up on the supply of goods; (b) a provision for the introduction of some capital by the investor; (c) area protection — not invariably given — and possibly options on additional areas. Further, the parent company may make a number of other services available to the investor — special training, the advantages of bulk purchasing and, in cases where the construction of premises is involved, help in site selection and the obtaining of permissions, the drawing up of plans and the supervision of building work.

The attraction of franchising is that it gives the investor the goodwill attached to an established name and the blueprint for an operation that is already proving successful elsewhere; but although there are a number of reputable and well-run parent companies in the franchising world, there also some that do not fall into either of these categories. Therefore, proceed with caution; and before you do anything else, consider whether a franchise of the type you are contemplating taking up makes commercial sense in the location being suggested. Insist on being given a list of several people already operating the same type of franchise and question all of them. Franchise salesmen can urge haste, but avoid paying deposits and make no commitment until you have completed your enquiries.

Be quite sure that your own ability and experience are appropriate to the project and that you will enjoy the type of work involved.

Your Bank Manager can obtain a Bank Reference and sometimes an informal opinion as well. Your Solicitor will explain the implications of the contract. Your Accountant will have a search made at Companies House on the parent company and will check projections and help with your personal cash flow and tax problems. They should all be consulted but the commercial decision will be yours because professional advisers must err on the side of caution. If you are a good negotiator you may secure better terms than those first offered.

The only organisation of which we have heard where you may be able to obtain an objective assessment of the project, help in negotiation and an opinion about the suitability for you personally is the Franchise Advisory Centre in London — but there may be others.

Government

There are many more vacancies for older people, i.e. over 35, than is generally realised both for 'permanent' and for 'temporary' posts with the Civil Service. Your study of newspaper advertisements in both the Offical Appointments columns and the Classified Display columns will soon tell you which skills are in demand and current rates of pay. For many posts regular 'competitions' are held (Administrative grade posts; Factory Inspectorate; Statisticians and Economists etc.) but applications may be considered at other times. In recent years the setting up of the prison industries has given openings for a large number of people with production expertise at almost any age (below 52). Some appointments are now on short-term contract — five years for example. As every post has to be advertised (either internally or externally or both) vacancies are not difficult to discover. General enquiries re the Civil Service should be addressed to:
The Civil Service Commission
Civil Service Department
Basingstoke, Hants

Local Government, both at County and Town Hall levels, is an area well worth considering for new career possibilities. Professionally qualified men — engineers, architects, solicitors

175

and so forth — are always in demand and salaries nowadays compare by no means unfavourably with the private sector. This is a field particularly worth looking at for men who have taken the academic part of a professional course — maybe through private study — but have not had the opportunity to complete the articles which enable them to practse professionally. Opportunities are, however, by no means confined to specialists. These days there is an increased appreciation of the kind of experience that a man with a good business background can bring to some of the Town Hall's more management-oriented activities, such as the administration of catering, entertainment and housing.

Another growth area in Local Government in recent years has been social and community work — the probation service, youth employment and organising the care of the old, the sick and the disadvantaged. It is a career that nowadays attracts a fair number of idealistic young graduates, but many local authorities would welcome a leavening of maturer men with a good all-round record and some experience of the world at large. Specialised training is, however, necessary. Fuller details of such schemes of the grants available can be obtained from The Social Work Advisory Centre, 26 Bloomsbury Way, London WC1A 2SR.

For information on Local Government appointments in general, write to the Clerk of the Council of the appropriate authority. With the recent reorganisation of Local Government into larger areas a new range of managerial skills is being demanded. Therefore the opportunities for people coming into Local Government from the outside are much greater than they have been hitherto and salaries nowadays are very competitive.

Lecturing and teaching
Some qualifications in this area are in greater demand than others — there is, for instance, a continuing shortage of personnel in maths and science. Lecturing jobs are advertised in the national press, but a good degree is usually a prerequisite. Those who are interested in teaching management and have the required academic qualifications and level of experience might consider the ten-week course

for prospective teachers of management studies at the Polytechnic, Regent Street, London W1. It costs £350 but you could, under certain circumstances, get a grant. The subject of 'Teaching in Technical Colleges' is more fully covered in a D.E.S. pamphlet of that name.

School teaching offers a wider range of opportunities, particularly to graduates or similarly qualified men and women. In most cases, though, a necessary preliminary to making a new career in this sphere would be to take a course (one year for graduates, two years for most non-graduates) at a College of Education. Grants are available to mature students and fuller details are available from the D.E.S. (Curzon Street, London W1) in two pamphlets, *Careers in Education for Graduates* and *Turn to Teaching*.

Opportunities in the Commonwealth

Apart from emigration — and there are considerable opportunities in the 'white' Commonwealth countries for first-class men with a British background — developing countries have a continuing need for experts to go out on longer-term contracts. The skills most in demand are high-level technical ones, such as engineering, construction work, works and production management and accountancy. Vacancies in the Commonwealth countries are often handled through the Overseas Development Administration of the Foreign and Commonwealth Office, Eland House, Stag Place, London. The International Recruitment Unit, at the same address, keeps a register of appointments in other developing countries.

Opportunities in the E.E.C.

In Continental Europe, as in the United Kingdom, there are opportunities for employment in both public and private sectors. The public sector usually means within the framework of the E.E.C., but in private industry also encompasses those European countries which are not members of the Community.

Public Sector

The openings that exist in public service can be taken to

177

include vacancies which occur at an official and semi-official level, such as within the E.E.C. Commission and Parliament themselves, U.N.E.S.C.O., N.A.T.O., C.E.R.N., E.S.R.O., and others. The majority of the positions that could be filled in this sector by British nationals include opportunities for linguistic secretaries, administrators (desirably linguistic, but not necessarily with a Civil Service background), translators and interpreters (who should be trilingual at least), teachers, and also for engineers and scientists within co-operative research establishments such as C.E.R.N. and E.S.R.O. Vacancies are usually advertised in the national press of the respective countries (including the U.K.), and applicants are normally invited to undergo a fairly exhaustive form-filling, testing and interviewing process. Success in this process can lead to a rewarding and financially comfortable career.

Private Sector
Employment opportunities in the private sector are much

more diverse and more difficult to define. It is comparatively rare at the moment for a French company operating in France to employ anyone but a Frenchman for an executive position, just as it is for a British company operating in Britain to employ anyone but a U.K. national for a similar post. Therefore, opportunities tend to be with the larger international companies (this usually means U.S.-based multinationals), and with the smaller organisations which earn their living from supplying services — such as management consultancy — to the international companies.

Linguistic requirements tend to vary greatly among the multinationals. English is invariably the business language of the U.S.-owned companies. But this is only. because the Americans are even more dilatory at learning languages than the British. As a result, the tendency is to recruit other managers and staff who do have a mastery of at least one other European language. This is not true, of course, of those U.S.-based multinationals which have their European headquarters in the United Kingdom, nor is it necessarily true for job functions in which communications depend on skills considered non-verbal, for example, accountancy or engineering. A broad hint of the requirements for U.K.-trained staff and management can be shown as follows:

Secretaries

Top-class British secretaries are in demand with international companies, particularly if trained in languages. This is well worth remembering for couples, or families, who wish to consider Europe.

Accountants

U.K.-trained Accountants (mainly Chartered, but also Cost and Management) are highly regarded for their professionalism both by Americans and by other Europeans. The major auditing firms in particular like to have British seniors on their staff. Languages are not usually necessary within the profession, but are helpful in industry.

Marketing/Sales Executives

Naturally, it would be unusual for local sales executives to be anything other than local nationals, but at sales and marketing management level it is fairly common to find a Briton, although he would normally need to have a very good command of at least one other major language. (For that reason, the Dutch and the Swiss, who tend to be multilingual, figure very prominently).

Technical

U.K.-trained engineers have a fairly strong contingent in the contracting industry connected with process plant and energy. This, however, is a 'closed shop', and most of the engineering personnel working in that industry are well aware of which companies in Europe can use their services. Other requirements for technical personnel from the U.K. depend on the availability of people within other countries – many U.S. organisations, particularly in electronics, have recently invested more time and money in other European countries than in the UK; nationals of those countries are sometimes better equipped technically and linguistically to compete in a modern international industry, hence Britons are in demand usually only when shortages of personnel occur – regrettably the belief that Britain has superior technological know-how is rapidly becoming a fallacy in many industries. In addition, the qualifications of H.N.C., or membership of one of the smaller Institutes is not recognised in the rest of Europe as conferring full engineer status, and many technical people from this country would find themselves working for, and receiving lower pay than, a less experienced but more highly qualified, colleague. The same principles apply to production management where, additionally, knowledge of local conditions and languages are absolutely essential.

Personnel Management

British personnel managers in fields such as recruitment and salary administration are quite well thought of, but, language knowledge is usually necessary. For positions in industrial relations, none but a national would be acceptable, except possibly at a senior strategic level.

Computer Personnel

Computer languages are universal, but spoken languages are usually also required.

General Management

There are several Britons holding top management positions within multinationals throughout Europe. But if you are this good sit back and wait for a headhunter to contact you!

Where, and which languages

The most popular cities for international companies to locate their European HQ's are Brussels and the Swiss cities such as Geneva and Zurich. Paris is less popular than it used to be (because of high commercial rents and a less inviting attitude taken in the De Gaulle era). German cities have increased in popularity, as have Dutch, while Luxemburg and Lichtenstein are attractive to corporations wishing to reduce tax liabilities; and the Casa per il Mezzogiorno (Commission for the development of the underdeveloped south) could reactivate interest in Italy.

It can be seen very quickly that French and German are useful languages to have, with Italian staging a comeback. However, new markets are being developed rapidly and Spanish, Portuguese and the Scandinavian languages might be the languages of the future. Eastern European languages have not yet come into their own and are not likely to do so for some time.

British and other European companies

With one or two exceptions, Continental European-based international companies are likely to employ Britons only for their British operations. Among the internationally-minded U.K. based companies, there is a growing trend to recruit multilingual accountants and marketing executives for work on acquisition projects, but once a company has been acquired there is still a tendency to retain local management, backed up by intermittent consultancy visits from the U.K. HQ team of accountants, marketing people and other disciplines as and when required.

Multinational management consultancy is a growing profession, principally in the areas of acquisitions, mergers and new product development, requiring financial, marketing, and linguistic expertise.

Where to look

There used to be a popular belief that tracking down daily copies of *Le Figaro* and *Die Frankfurter Allgemeine* was the best way of finding a job in France or Germany. In reality, if any company, whether American, German or British, wishes to advertise for a U.K. executive it will probably use a British newspaper such as *The Daily Telegraph, Sunday Times, Financial Times* or *The Economist* (which also carries job ads for the public sector). The possible exception is in Brussels where *The Bulletin* is a weekly magazine published for the English-speaking communities. In addition to recruitment advertisements, it also carries advertisements for accommodation and other such domestic matters.

There are a few U.K.-based employment agents and selection consultants with contacts in Europe, but employment agents as such are illegal in most European countries. There are, however, many search and selection firms in most large international towns, and a glance through the local 'yellow pages' (if readily obtainable) will provide a few names and addresses. If you enclose a covering letter with your c.v., you may not receive a reply, but if you do it will probably say that a register of applicants is not maintained (as this is illegal); your details will be kept on file and you will be contacted should a suitable opportunity occur (which, in fact, they sometimes do!). Beware of consultants, of any nationality, who offer to package, market and place you, then charge you a fee for it. They should already be charging their client companies a fair sum.

Other sources worth trying are the Commercial Attachés of U.S. Embassies of relevant countries. They may be able to supply a list of American companies with operations in those countries.

Of the directories, the most useful sets are *Kompass* for each country, and *Who Owns Whom* (U.K. and North American editions) which, between them, should give you a comprehensive list of British, American and Canadian companies with operations in Europe, indicating also what those operations are.

Finally, it is important to bear in mind that any applications or general enquiries made in writing should contain a detailed c.v., laid out logically and chronologically, and should include a passport-type photograph.

The main differences
Many of the difficulties embodied in a different way of

working and living can be overcome if the following points are considered beforehand:

1. Is this the correct step to take as part of a career strategy? Many British executives have returned home after two or three years (for many different reasons) to find they are unable to command the high salaries earned in Europe, but unwilling to accept less. One major multinational group has in fact, suspended the recruitment of executives from the U.K. until a more far-reaching management development policy has been researched and instigated.

2. Do not sell your U.K. home — rent it out. It would be tragic to find that, should you wish to return home after a few years, you are priced out of the U.K. housing market. It is much more unusual and more difficult to purchase property on the Continent than it is here.

3. If you have a family, is the local education system acceptable to you? There are many excellent schools in Europe, but the accent on academic attainment is sometimes greater than in Britain, with the resultant loss of other aspects of education.

4. Is the social environment such that your wife will feel at home, and be able to develop her own career or interest?

5. Lastly, it should be stated that most North European executives work longer hours and spend more time away from home than do their British counterparts. Also, they are better rewarded (50% more for a comparable job in the U.K. is a reasonable figure to expect), and, in most countries, enjoy a more favourable tax rate and more comprehensive benefits.

It is difficult to summarise what the chances are of making a successful move, but the results of a survey made recently of Britons working in Europe indicated that nearly 70% were satisfied and did not contemplate a return in the foreseeable future.

These are just some of the opportunities you might consider if you want to strike out in a fresh direction. One final word about this. Whatever you decide to do talk it over thoroughly with your wife and your older children. It is not easy to switch in mid-career. It may involve sacrifices, uncertainty, even a drop in what you have considered to be your status. The burden will fall on your family as much as on you. If they are not behind you — and they may not be if they feel something has been forced down their throats — you are placing a handicap on yourself that could mean the difference between success and failure.

Appendix A:
Writing 'on-spec' letters

Almost every managing director has one or two 'on-spec' letters addressed to him each week. Usually he glances at them and then asks his secretary to pass them on to a subordinate; from where they usually go into one of those files that are seldom, if ever, referred to. But a letter that shows you are alert to what the company you are writing to is doing is much more likely to arouse the recipient's attention; if only for the simple and human reason that we all tend to be interested in people who show an interest in us.

For instance, you may have read a business news item where an engineering company has bought a controlling interest in a German firm as part of its Common Market policy. Before long this company will be needing people in various capacities who speak German and who have a knowledge of the special problems and opportunities of operating in a Common Market country. If you have qualifications of this sort to offer your letter is likely to produce an interview even if the company concerned has not yet got around to considering what new staff it needs to handle the problems its acquisition is going to pose.

Let us take the hypothetical case of a personnel man, aged 47 or so, with a degree in German. He has always taken an interest in the labour situation in his industry as it applies in Germany, has kept abreast of the main books and articles on the subject that have appeared over there and has written the occasional piece on the subject – perhaps in a professional journal – and has talked about it to his local Chamber of Commerce or at conferences. In other words, he is not expert but he knows enough to get by and has something specific to point to. A sample letter to a company chairman or managing director might look something like this.

Dear Sir X,

I noticed in your company report in the *Financial Times* on the 17th March that your firm has recently bought a controlling interest in Süddeutsche Metallwerke GmbH. I imagine that you will be retaining the existing German management, but it occurs to me that before long you may be bringing in new policies which will require close, knowledgeable and sympathetic liaison with your German staff. As an experienced personnel manager with a degree in German and a special knowledge of German labour laws and negotiation machinery (on which I have written a number of articles) I feel I might be of particular use to you; and I for my part am looking for a job that will enable me to apply my interest in comparative British and German approaches to personnel problems in a practical way.

May I come and talk to you about the possibilities? I look forward to hearing from you.

Apart from the fact that a letter like this makes it clear that (a) the applicant it taking an intelligent interest in the company he is writing to and (b) has something concretely useful to offer them, it embodies a number of other lessons which are pertinent to the 'on-spec' approach.

1. It is fairly short, but it covers the salient points and offers enough specific information about the applicant to arouse the reader's interest.
2. It does not give away the applicant's age — there is plenty of time to do that when it is asked for.
3. It does not specifically say whether or not the applicant is currently in a job. If you are not working, do not volunteer this information. (On the other hand, if you are this is a plus point and should always be brought in. But do not do so too obtrusively, otherwise the cynical reader may assume that you have been asked to 'look around'!)
4. It concludes with a firm, but polite request for action on the part of the recipient.

The point of such a letter is that while it does not include a résumé it arouses enough interest for one to be requested. This has two important advantages over the 'out of the blue' approach. First of all, having asked for a résumé, the recipient will read it, which he might not have done had it come unsolicited. Secondly, if the reader has asked you to do something — namely, prepare a full résumé — he will usually feel under some obligation to you, the least manifestation of which would be to ask you to come for an interview, whereas otherwise your age might not get you over this all-important first hurdle. Once you are in, you are in with a chance.

The example we have given is, of course, a very 'soft-sell' approach. A marketing man approaching other marketing men might want to use something with more punch. Like this, for instance:

Dear Mr. Smith,

I notice in *The Caterer and Hotelkeeper* of the 3rd June that AB Foods are planning to launch a new kind of vending machine, for providing self-service in hotel bedrooms. I am keen to make a move into a sphere with some real growth potential, which I feel sure this has, but apart from that I have a good deal of very relevant experience to offer you in this new venture. I started off my business career in catering and was Assistant Manager of the Grand Hotel in Aberdeen before being lured away into selling. Most recently I was regional manager in the Midlands for Peter Lorraine's wines division. I was in charge of a team of eighteen representatives and during my time there sales rose from £250,000 to close on a million. On the ideas side, I might say it was at my suggestion that the company launched its very successful scheme of selling wine from the cask in off-licences.

May I come and see you to discuss how I can help you? I shall phone your secretary next week to find out when you are free to make a date.

The last sentence puts a foot – albeit a tactful one – in the door and would probably not be suitable if you were writing for an administrative post. But here the writer is looking for a job that involves selling and his positive attitude suggests that he is not a man who readily takes no for an answer. Notice, though, that underneath the slightly brash tone the letter is still quite specific about what the applicant has to offer in the way of experience and achievement. On the other hand, it does not go into too much detail, because the object is to whet the reader's appetite rather than to tell him the whole story. This has the further advantage that it enables you to be selective — to talk about the highlights without mentioning any troughs that might have occurred. Those will, of course, have to come later, at the interview or when you are asked to submit a résumé (though you should avoid volunteering information about why you left this or that job). But as any mail order man can tell you, once interest in a product has been aroused at all the first important step towards making a sale has already been taken.

Writing an effective 'on-spec' letter is a task that should not be underrated, even by those who are accustomed to expressing themselves in writing. It is a good idea, when you have prepared such a letter, to put it away for a few days and then look at it again with fresh eyes. Even better, though, is to show your letter to a friend whose judgement you trust. Don't ask him for a general opinion — which is likely to produce a general sort of answer that may err on the side of politeness — but for replies to specific questions about its effectiveness. Here are some points to check.

1. *Have you clearly identified the reason why you are writing?*

Beware of making your approach so oblique and 'soft-sell' that the reader is left in doubt about what you are getting at. At some point you should specifically put over the fact that you are looking for a job with the firm to whom you are writing.

2. *Is your letter likely to arouse the recipient's interest and attention almost as soon as he starts reading it?*

The best way to do this, as we have said earlier, is to appeal to his self-interest by identifying a need which you think he has or might have and showing how you can fill it. For instance, every firm has middle-management problems, needs accountants, looks for people with a proven record of sales success. As an executive you will know general personnel problems in your area of experience even if you cannot find the need that particularly applies to the firm you are writing to.

3. *Does it omit unnecessary data that will make it too long to read?*

Bear in mind that the recipient is a busy man. He has a lot of letters on his desk that he has to read and answer.

4. *Does your letter clearly imply that you are a forward-looking man with an open mind and plenty to contribute for the future?*

Cut out phrases that sound as though you are an old dog who can't be taught any new tricks ('a lifetime of experience in the ... business'). Emphasise what you achieve in the job, not how long you did it for.

5. *Is the writing crisp, precise and easy to follow?*

Avoid pompous words (beware particularly of those of latin origin), long involved sentences, repetitions and near-repetitions of meaning or content.

6. *Does each sentence, and each paragraph follow logically from the one before it?*

First of all, the letter must have an overall structure. It must have a beginning (why you are writing), a middle (a thumbnail sketch of your qualifications and experience), and an end (request for an interview). That is one way to lay out the contents, and probably the best one. But whichever method you choose, don't go hopping back and forth with details that are not related to each other or which are not obviously connected. In the examples we have just given, for instance, it would be rather puzzling at first reading if the writer had put: 'I started off my business career in catering and was assistant manager of the Grand Hotel in Aberdeen. Latterly I was regional manager etc.' Notice how he has linked the two jobs together with the phrase 'before being lured into selling'.

7. *Is the spelling, punctuation and grammar correct?*

You may think this is unnecessary advice, but a lot of people slip into errors, just as one tends to slip into bad driving habits: it gets you there but it doesn't follow the book. To some people who read letters of application mistakes in strictly correct English (e.g. not knowing when to put its or it's) are irritating. If you're not sure of a word, look it up.

8. *If you're writing to someone by name, have you got the spelling right?*

Appendix B:
Guidelines for preparing your c.v.

A c.v. is a factual summary of you and your career to date. It can be used for any appointment when supplemented by information specific to that job. Try to keep your summary to one page (or at most two pages), if possible, following the order set out below.

Full Name
Address
Telephone Number — Home   — Office
Date of Birth
Nationality
Marital Status
Education (dates, type of school/college, location and principal examinations, subjects and results)
Languages
Professional Qualifications
Military Service
Career Summary (what jobs you have held and what you consider to be your most significant achievement).
Publications
Other Appointments/Achievements (e.g. J.P., Member of National Export Council 19— to 19—)
Remuneration in present/most recent job (give basic salary plus bonus, special fringe benefits)
Period of Notice (i.e. when you would be available — omit this if not currently employed).

It is the practice of many firms and consultants to verify academic/professional qualifications and membership of professional bodies, at the short-list stage. To avoid unnecessary delay, ensure that the information you give includes the exact name of the university/professional institution, with dates and degree/membership levels.

Appendix C:
Specimen letter of application in reply
to an advertised vacancy

257 Spring Gardens,
Cookley,
Surrey.

1st February 1974

Dear Sir,

I wish to apply for the post (advertised in the Daily Telegraph of the 30th January) of Marketing Director of English International Airlines Limited and enclose my curriculum vitae.

I have had extensive experience in civil aviation, mostly operational, with an ever-increasing amount of administration and have taken full advantage of courses in order to further my knowledge.

My current post is in the contract department of Southern Airlines at Gatwick, where all types of services are provided for international flag carriers, charter airlines, corporate aircraft and private aviation. With the recent increase in private small plane movements at the airport, we have been quick to realise the potential and hold a virtual monopoly in the handling of this business.

The unit has diversified over the past two years to embrace private and business operators and I have been closely concerned with negotiating and initiating methods and procedures to provide the individual service this type of customer requires.

I am commercially minded and believe in 'selling' our service vigorously. Last year I represented the company at the Business and Light Aircraft Show at Cranfield, where we secured a lot of new business. The current climate in civil aviation has made me economically minded and I have made

191

several suggestions to my Managing Director for cost cutting, many of which have been implemented.

I have had dealings with all levels of people in aviation, civil and military, plus the Department of Trade and Industry, Customs, Immigration and other statutory bodies.

I welcome the opportunity to become a member of a small company and know that my experience and knowledge will be beneficial to English International Airlines and that my ideas for expansion in the future are valuable. I am very ambitious and dedicated to aviation and know that I am the man your Chairman, Group Captain Tom Higgins, is seeking to guide his company into a profitable and successful future. I believe that the potential of this type of company is enormous and look forward to being a part of that future.

Yours faithfully,

Q.S. Silver

Notes on how this letter has been constructed

Para 1. States the name of the post being applied for. Remember a company may be advertising more than one executive post at any one time!

Para 2. Gives a thumbnail picture, in one sentence, of the nature of the applicant's experience.

Para 3. Describes what the applicant is doing in his current appointment and shows how this relates to the job being advertised.

Para 4. Covers his experience in the immediate past, again making it clear how this relates to a marketing appointment.

Para 5. The applicant says something about the kind of person he is and backs it up with specific evidence of achievement.

Para 6. Describes the range and nature of his contacts.

Para 7. A vigorous and positive conclusion is reinforced by the fact that the applicant has managed to dig up the name of the company's chairman. It is therefore likely that he has taken the trouble to find out something about the company as a whole.

Appendix D:
Useful sources of information

Basic information on all companies has to be lodged with the Registrar of Companies (Companies House, 55 City Road, London EC1) and is available for inspection by members of the public. It will show the latest account, the balance sheet and the names, qualifications and place of birth of the directors. Charges against assets, such as mortgages, also have to be shown.

Public reference libraries in large cities, as well as the libraries of leading professional associations and institutes (such as the B.I.M. and the I.P.M.), carry a variety of reference works that can help you in your search and give you useful background information for interviews. Some of the principal works that may be worth consulting are listed below.

Moodies British Companies Index will give you extracts of annual reports and chairmen's statements; profit record; share price movement; and a host of other information on companies' activities.

The Kompass Register covers some 28,000 British firms, identifying them by products and services and describing in tabular form what sort of trading activities they undertake.

Dun & Bradstreet's Guide to Key British Enterprises lists several thousands of British companies, showing the address, type of activity, when founded, names of directors and the sales turnover.

Dun & Bradstreet's British Middle Market Directory is a companion volume providing similar information for 'the progressive middle sector of British industry and commerce'.

Dun & Bradstreet's International Market Guides gives names, addresses, products and services of companies in many of the leading industrial companies of the world. Frequently also, financial appraisals of these companies are provided.

Standard and Poor's Corporation Research gives details of the activities of the 6,000 largest U.S. firms.

The Times 1,000 List of Companies: company reports are kept on file at most reference libraries.

Extel Statistical Services are a source of financial information on both quoted and unquoted British companies. There is also the *Extel European Service,* which extends mainly to quoted European companies.

London Gazette gives information about bankruptcies and the people involved in them. Back numbers are obviously useful for checking the credentials of people or firms you feel doubtful about.

Research Index – Companies Section appears fortnightly and is therefore very up-to-date on company news and financial information.

Who Owns Whom lists and cross indexes parent companies, their subsidiaries and associates.

The British Technology Index is an index to all business and commercial journals for all subject areas.

The Directory of British Associations lists trade associations and chambers of commerce.

Special business surveys and supplements, both of countries and specific industries are undertaken from time to time by the leading national newspapers. The publisher's library will be able to tell you whether they have any recent surveys on any particular field. The *Economist Intelligence Unit* is particularly good in this area.

Directories, Yearbooks and Annuals can be a valuable source of information. *The Stock Exchange Yearbook,* for instance, gives a thumbnail financial picture of all quoted public companies. Another well-known publication, the advertisers' *Blue Book* lists market research, direct mail and PR firms, as well as showing agencies and their clients.

Management Courses in the U.K. is a select guide to courses, describing what they do and how long they take.

British Qualifications is a comprehensive survey of all qualifications in Britain, how they are obtained and through whom. It also tells you what all those letters after people's names mean — useful in interviews. Published by Kogan Page.

Index of Advertisers

Alangate Vocational Counselling Service   89

Anglian Regional Management Centre   173
(North East London Polytechnic)

Ashley Associates   120

Boyden International Ltd   111

Bristol Polytechnic (South West Regional   117
Management Centre)

Career Analysts   111

Criterion Appointments Ltd   112

Daily Telegraph, Marketing Division   Bookmark

Euroselection   178

Executive Care   89

John Figes and Partners Ltd   65, 112

Franchise Advisory Centre Ltd   112, 173

Graduate Appointments Registers   113

Korn-Ferry Dickinson Ltd   8

Lansdowne Appointments Register   87, 113

Management On The Move Ltd   113

Management Personnel   114

Charles Martin Associates Ltd   114

North East London Polytechnic   173
(Anglian Regional Management Centre)

Graeme Odgers and Co Ltd   115

Richard Owen Associates   115

Portsmouth Management Centre   118

South West Regional Management Centre   117
(Bristol Polytechnic)

Stroud Morgan   65, 115

Talent Brokers   116

Western Men International   116

Western Personnel Ltd   119